'Here the needle plies its busy task;
The pattern grows, the well depicted flower,
Wrought patiently into the snowy lawn,
Unfolds its bosom; buds, and leaves, and sprigs,
And curling tendrils, gracefully dispos'd,
Follow the nimble fingers of the fair—
A wreath that cannot fade, of flowers that blow
With most success when all besides decay.'

From *The Winter Evening* by William Cowper

New Design in Bobbin Lace

ANN COLLIER

B. T. Batsford · London

ISBN   0 7134 4215 8

Typeset by Latimer Trend & Company Ltd, Plymouth
and printed in Great Britain by
Anchor Brendon Ltd
Tiptree, Essex
for the publishers
B. T. Batsford Ltd
4 Fitzhardinge Street
London W1H 0AH

Contents

Acknowledgements

Much of the lace in this book has been designed and worked by myself but I should like to thank Eeva Lisa Kortalahti from Finland, and Annemarie Rager and Marie Jeanne Cooreman from Belgium for allowing me to use some of their designs. My thanks also to Marie Vankova Kuchynkova and other Czech lace artists for allowing me to use photographs of their work, and to my students Jean Spindlow and Margaret Lewis for checking the text.

Introduction to design

The technique of bobbin lace imposes certain limitations on design; these can be used to produce interesting effects. Several things govern your approach to design: the final use of the lace, the required shape, the technique to be used, the final mounting and the colour. It is advisable to have these decided before designing and planning the stitches. Lacemakers are essentially making a piece of woven material which will support itself, unlike embroidery which requires a backing material.

Designs can be naturalistic – animals, birds, flowers, etc. – or they can be stylized and given a more decorative appearance. Some shapes can be so simplified that they become symbolic or even abstract; others can be geometric and rely on the structural patterns formed by the lace. These geometric designs are the easiest; their regularity makes them suitable for Torchon or Point ground and it is only when curves are introduced that difficulty arises. This can be overcome by using different angles of graph paper or working the design out by eye. Many Honiton lacemakers of the past put in their fillings by eye, a more realistic result with none of the problems produced by a graphed ground, such as the need to use half patterns.

In one-piece lace one has to use all the threads to make a pleasing pattern; they hold the lace together and make the pattern continuous. Motif laces like Honiton, Bruges and Duchesse can be worked with as many threads as one likes and so the planning is simpler. A combination of both methods is often the best way to accomplish a pictorial design.

The following chapters show various ways of producing designs with the various forms of lace. There is special emphasis on the uses of lace. Many of the patterns need to be enlarged to make them workable so for the most part no thread is mentioned. Some can be made small, worked in Honiton but most of these patterns have been made with Sylko which is readily available.

Fig. 1   *Twisted braids and scroll*

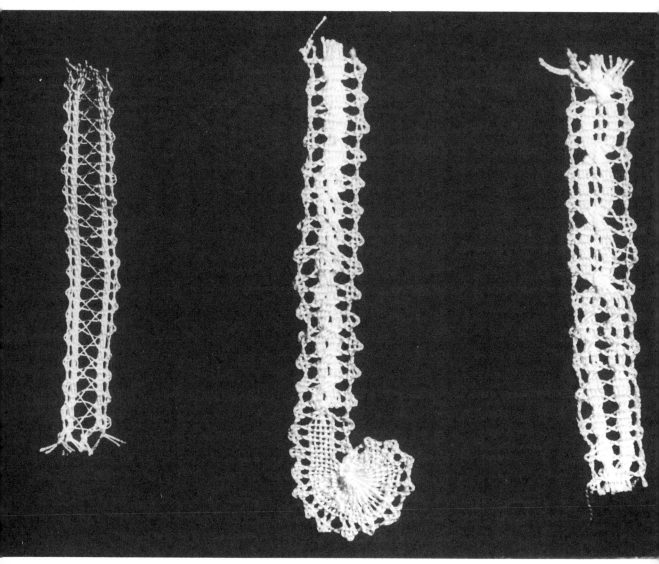

ONE

Tape lace

One of the easiest forms of bobbin lace is braid or tape, as it requires only a few bobbins and by making it twist and turn, any shape can be achieved. It has the advantage of simplicity and colour can be easily used. Its disadvantage is that it is very repetitive and can be boring to do. Variations of stitch can make it more interesting and here there seems to be unlimited scope. Twists in the passives and weavers can spread it and give surface interest; embellishments such as holes and raised tallies can give it texture; the use of thin and thick threads can give dimension; and with two half stitches worked in the centre of a cloth stitch braid, it becomes much more lace-like. A very interesting effect can be achieved by crossing the passives in a braid rather like the cables in Aran knitting.

Twisted braids (Diag. 1 and Fig. 1)

1. This requires nine pairs. Work with a foot and weave through all the pairs from right to left in cloth stitch. Lift three pairs of passives on the right over the three pairs on the left so that they change places and form a ridge as in Aran cables (do not weave them through one another). Weave through in cloth stitch from left to right and continue in this way. The pin holes for the braid will be further apart than normal to accommodate the crossings.

2. This has nine pairs as in *1* but each time, the weaver is worked through three pairs, twisted and then worked through the other three pairs.

3. This has ten pairs. Work through three pairs, twist, through one pair, twist, through three pairs. The weaver passes through three times before each crossing of the passives.

4. A double cable has one set crossed right over left and the other crossed left over right with twists as shown.

Turning braids

The technique of turning a braid neatly by the Flemish method is by far the easiest. Any braid however rounded can turn and pivot on one pin for as many times as it takes to round the bend and level out again. It can be worked in cloth stitch, half stitch or cloth and twist. Work to pin *A* (see Diag. 2) and back to outer pin *B*, work back to within one pair of *A*, twist the weavers, take them behind the pin and under the passive pair at *A*. Weave back to *B*. Repeat this until the curve is complete. Take out the pin at *A* and sew the passive pair into the first loop, replace the pin and continue the braid. You will notice on removal of the

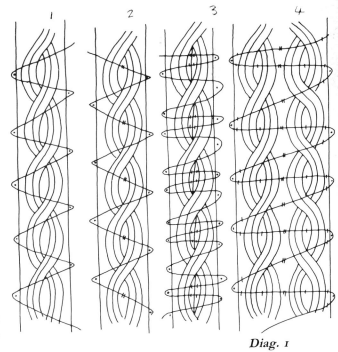

Diag. 1

9

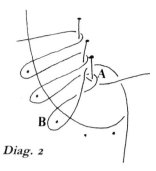

Diag. 2

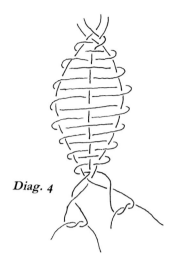

Diag. 4

pin that the passive pair acts as a gathering thread which holds all the threads together without bulk. This method can be used for scrolls or for complete rounds.

A round (flower 1)

This can be achieved by pivoting on a central pin and making the complete round in cloth and twist (Diag 3). The twists in the passives need to be adjusted to keep the wheel formation, four on the outside, three, two, one to the centre. Begin by having the pairs on

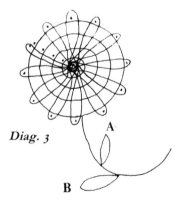

Diag. 3

the line of pin holes marked, pivot on the centre one, work round and sew out the pairs in their relevant places. Sew in the pivot pair to the centre and tie it off with the adjacent pair. This round can make a flower by using the sewn-in threads to make a stalk in stem stitch. The leaves can be made with two pairs from *A* worked into the stem and dropped out at *B*. The threads of the leaf can be tied off and threaded back.

To tie a plaited leaf

Place the weaving thread back in its original position, tie the two opposite threads in a single overhand, then tie the weaver and the other (Diag. 4). This holds the leaf firm and stops the distortion that sometimes occurs; it can be used to tie off tallies or leadworks.

Flower 2

This flower has a centre worked as for the round, but leave two pairs on the tie edge tied off but not cut off (Diag. 5). Use these to make Maltese leaves in and out of the centre. Make the stalk as in Flower 1 (above). Flowers like these can be made in various sizes (Fig. 2) and with different centres to decorate lampshades and household linen. They can also be given wire stalks to make three-dimensional daisies for corsages or bouquets.

A simple use for tape lace is in calligraphy decorations for dresses, bags, paperweights etc. The simplest form consists of flowing, hand-written letters as in Diag. 6. The secret is to have as continuous a line as possible. These shown can be enlarged for whatever purpose and can be further decorated with Flower 1 or 2.

The second alphabet is a Roman one. Directions are given for the letter 'R' because it has all the features and workings of the other letters. It could be used for a child's picture, with the train and perhaps the child's name picked out in colour.

Diag. 5

Diag.

Fig. 2 *Different sizes of petalled flower with various centres*

Fig. 3 *Simple twisted braid 'A' decorated with a flower*

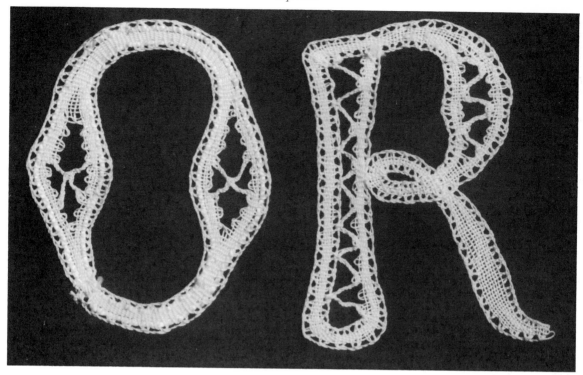

Letter 'R'

Fig. 4 *Detail of alphabet*

Start at *A* in Diag. 7 with four pairs and increase on every row to eight, curve round with sewings at *B* and divide the braid at *C*. Work both sides simultaneously, adding two pairs at *D*. These pairs form the plait which is taken into the braids from side to side and finally absorbed at *E*. Join the braids at *F* and begin to reduce pairs to seven. Continue the braid with these to *G*, add two pairs and plait from side to side, taking them in on one side and sewing in on the other. Sew out finally at *H*. This method of combining sewings with working in one piece makes the lace stronger and neater. The other letters can be worked in a similar way using Fig. 3 as a guide. Fig. 5 shows a complete alphabet.

The train

A simple braid forms the basic shape with fillings inserted afterwards to make an interesting inner; the threads are carried through as much as possible. Refer to Diag. 8. Start at *A* on the slant line with six pairs and work a simple braid to *A*. Sew out but leave two pairs not cut off, to work the filling. Sew in eight pairs along *C* and work a half stitch braid to *DE*, tie out and cut off all but two pairs, use these for leaf *E*. Make plaits and leaves to *B*, sew out and cut off. Sew in two

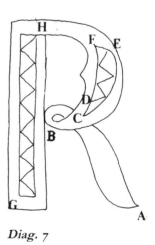

Diag. 7

Fig. 5 *Complete Roman alphabet*

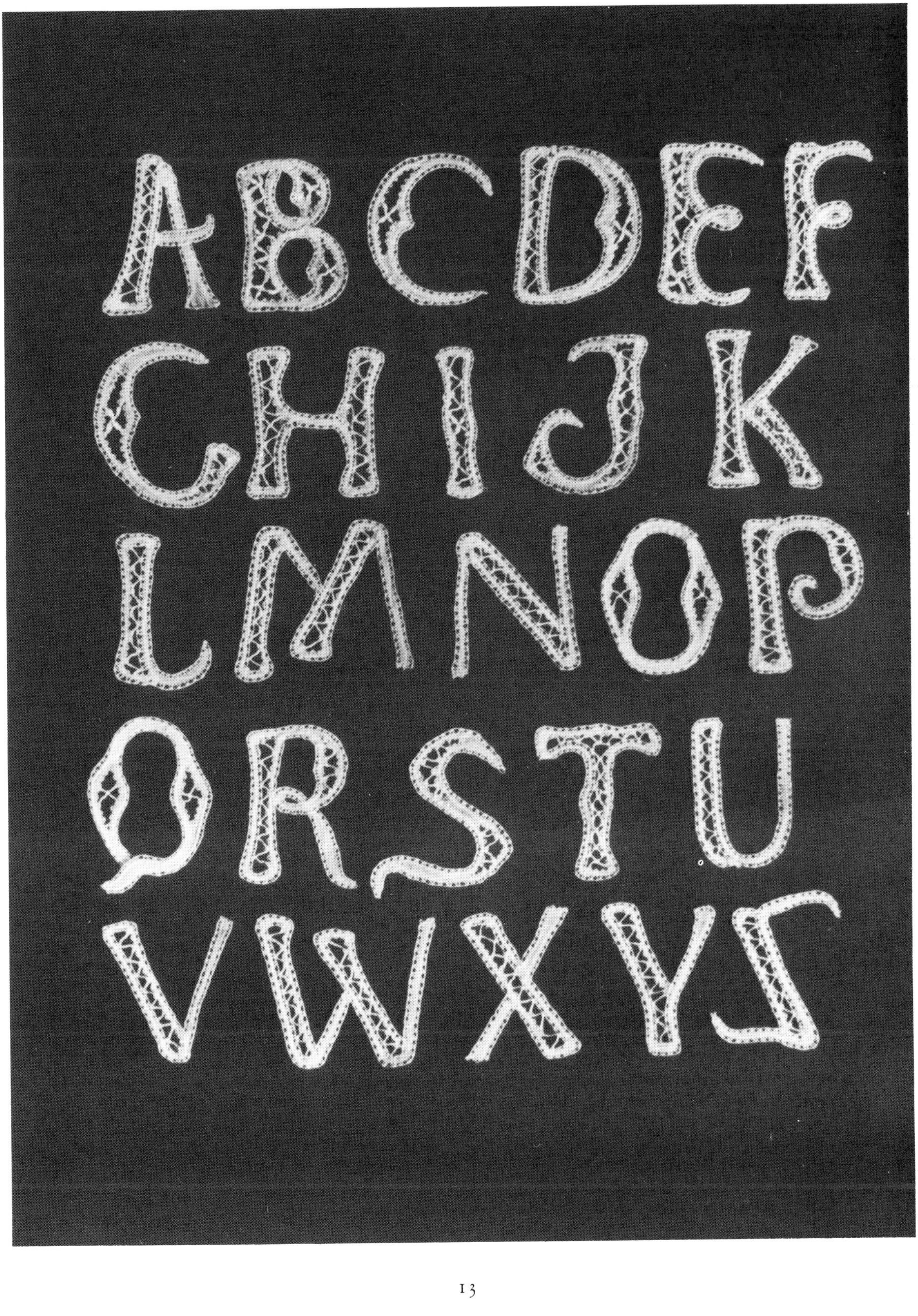

Fig. 6 *Tape lace train and carriage*

Diag. 8

pairs at *F* and *G* and make the flower with a six-pair crossing in the centre. Sew out four pairs, leaving two pairs to plait to the second flower. Sew in pairs at *H* and *I* and work the second flower with a half stitch centre. Sew out and leave two pairs for the third flower. Sew in pairs at *J* and *K*, work flower, sew out at *L* and plait to *M*, and from *N* to *O*. Work half stitch smoke from *P* to *Q* and use the pairs to make the leaves in the funnel. Make wheels in rounds, turning on the centre pin and sewing in to the train.

The carriage

Begin the braid at *A* in Diag. 9 and sew out at *B*. Sew in two pairs on each place from *C* to *D*. Work plaits and crossings as shown and use these to make the half stitch windows and door. Work these simultaneously, keeping one pair to link the windows and sides. Work flowers as before and complete the wheels. Figs 5 and 6 show the engine and carriage complete.

Waterlily inset

This pattern (Diag. 10 and Fig. 7) forms a round of four repeats and can be used as an inset to a dress or

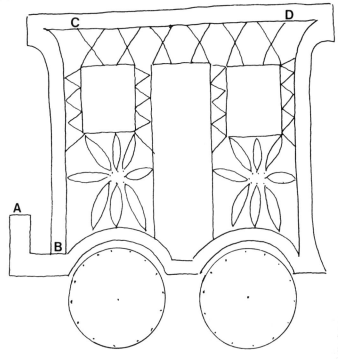

Diag. 9

blouse, in a circular cloth, as an edge to a circular mat or as a collar. It consists of three braids joined with sewings and the use of twists or half stitch will widen the braid when necessary.

Work Braid A first in any fancy way, crossed threads, with centre half stitch etc. Braid B consists of alternating cloth and half stitch with sewings down the centres of the petals and to Braid A. The four leaves at *D* are worked in conjunction with the braid taking them in and out as shown. Braid C is worked in four sections, starting each at *C* and sewing out at *M*. It overlaps Braid B and is sewn in as in crossing braids. The small braid at *N* with three plaits starting at *O* is worked afterwards using single pairs sewn in at *P*, *Q* and *R*, then tied out on the opposite side. The flower at *F* is also worked after completion by sewing in at *E*, *F*, *G* and *H*, working a half stitch centre and sewing out at *I*, *J*, *K*, and *L*.

Fig. 7 *Waterlily inset for a dress with a back opening*

Continuous line designs

Some of the continuous line designs from Islam can be used with little alteration. Diag. 11 has two braids worked simultaneously, crossing one another as shown. They would be effective on dress, furnishings or lampshades.

Diag. 12 makes an interesting inset, a paperweight or (in metallic threads) a necklace. Begin at *A* and finish at *B*.

Diag. 10

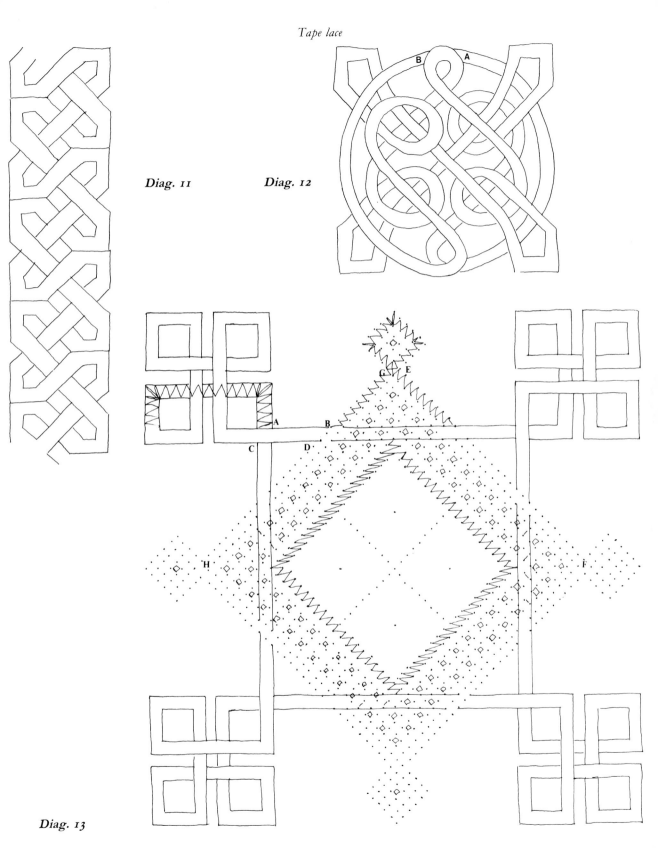

Tape lace

Diag. 11   Diag. 12

Diag. 13

Islam panel

This can be enlarged for a cushion 30 cm by 30 cm. Three panels 20 cm by 20 cm make a lampshade. Refer to Diag. 13 and Fig. 8.

Start a braid at *A* and another at *B*, work them simultaneously so that they cross one another alternately, sew in at *C* and *D*. The threads for the rose ground are sewn in from *E* to *F* and from *G* to *H*. Work the torchon panel in the centre in rose ground and spiders, sewing in to and crossing the other braids where necessary. Sew out at the base. Pin stitch the panel to the material before making up. The material behind the rose ground can be cut away.

Note. To keep the continuity of the rose ground some of the rose squares have to be adjusted – these lie unseen behind the braid.

Fig. 8 *Islamic design for a lampshade*

TWO

Three-dimensional flowers & insects

Three-dimensional models of flowers and insects can be used as brooches and bouquets, in decorative pictures or as delicate sculptures under glass domes.

Naturalistic flowers

These are made in one piece as tape lace with sewings as the basic element in the design, making the veins and open areas as in Honiton lace. Flowers fall into several categories according to their shape: daisies with multiple-pointed petals and flat middles; daffodils with trumpets; roses with heart-shaped petals; and orchids which have a combination of petals of different shapes. Most of the flowers which can be successfully made in lace fall into these groupings.

Each part of the flower is worked and then assembled, and it is a good idea to take a flower apart and observe its construction, colour, shading, and petal shape, and above all to see how to interpret it as a flattened shape. Each part of the flower needs to be worked to create a natural effect: petals, centre parts, calyx and leaves. They can be made in their natural colour but look infinitely better in white or cream with just a hint of their natural colour, or in very pale shades of it. They are better in a fine thread, such as Sylko 50, and are very effective in silk as a sheen can be created. They are improved by using fine fuse wire (wound on to bobbins) as a gimp. This enables one to curve the petals into a realistic shape.

Daisies

The continuous braid can be worked in several different ways: these have been shown in Diag. 14a on one flower, so trace off the entire flower with the desired working. The petals can all be the same, or they can alternate.

Begin at *A* with six pairs plus wire and one thread as its pair. Cloth-stitch to the tip, turn on a pin until level and change to half stitch. Continue in this way back to *A*, sew out.

Petal B has five pairs plus wire. Begin at *B* and work down to the tip, leave out one pair at *C* and a pair at *D*. Cross these pairs with a cloth stitch and take in and drop out on one side, and sew in and drop out on the other back to *B*.

Petal E is worked as for Petal B but instead of a simple crossing of the pairs, a tally or leadwork is made or a bead sewn in and continued as for Petal B.

Petal F has four pairs plus wire, worked as for Petal B but two pairs added at *G, H* and *I*. Work leaves and stalk making three plait crossings where necessary, and sewing in and out as in Petal B.

A multiple-petalled daisy can be made by making several of these and combining them all together with the centre when making up.

Diag. 14a

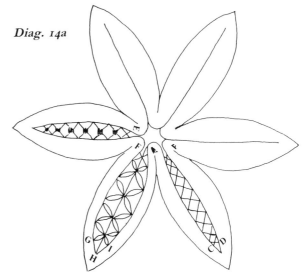

Fig. 9 *Three-dimensional daisy*

Assembly

Take a suitably sized button and push some florist's wire through the holes of the button as in Diag. 16. Put a gathering thread round the spider centre and place over the button, add a small amount of cotton wool to cover the button and make the middle raised. Sew into place, pull the wire and button middle through the petal centre or centres and again sew into place. Slide on the calyx and holding the whole assembly, firmly bind the stalk wire with green or white tape of the type available from florists.

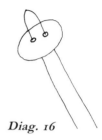

Diag. 16

Daisy centre

Start at *A* by laying the threads of four pairs behind *B* as in Diag. 14c, and having two pairs on *A*. Weave from *A* to *B* and from *A* to *C*, thus starting both sides of the circle at the same time. Work both sides simultaneously adding pairs on either side to work the spider ground. Take these pairs out into the edge and use or discard as is necessary to complete the circle. Tie off the pairs where they meet at the end – this will not show as it is hidden by the petals. Beads can be added to the spider centres to give a raised effect. Make a calyx (Diag. 15) with four pairs if desired; this will cover the ends of thread from the petals and centre.

Daffodil

Work a six-petal as in the daisy, with any combination of pattern.

Trumpet (no wire)

Begin at *A* with four pairs and increase on every pin to *B* in half stitch. Leave a pair out on every pin from *B* to *C* decreasing again to four pairs. Turn and work a fancy edge with these four pairs either in a stem-stitch picot rib as in Honiton or working a fan edge as in Diag. 17. This edge is sewn into the half stitch where shown and sewn out and tied off at *A*.

Assembly

Attach a few stamens to a doubled wire stalk. Fold over the trumpet to form a cone using the cast-out threads to sew and join. Push the stalk through the trumpet and then the trumpet through the petals. Stitch lightly and then, holding firmly, bind the end of the trumpet and the stalk with tape. Fig. 10 shows the complete flower.

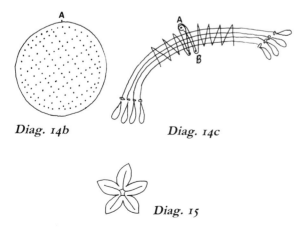

Diag. 14b   **Diag. 14c**

Diag. 15

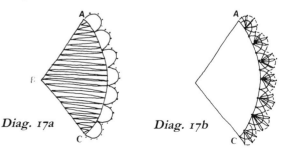

Diag. 17a   **Diag. 17b**

Fig. 10   *Daffodil*

Fig. 11   *Narcissus*

Snowdrop

Work only three petals and join them to form a cone. Insert the trumpet further into the petals and bind as before.

Narcissus

Work trumpet as for the daffodil but with petals as in Diag. 18. These are more rounded and worked in half stitch. The turning on a pin is much wider giving more threads round the pin. This forms a very pleasing pattern on the petal. Assemble as for the daffodil but push the trumpet further into the petals. There will be more of the trumpet pushed into the stem. Fig. 11 shows the complete flower.

You can give the trumpet coloured edges by introducing a coloured pair as the weaver.

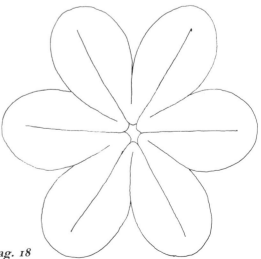

Diag. 18

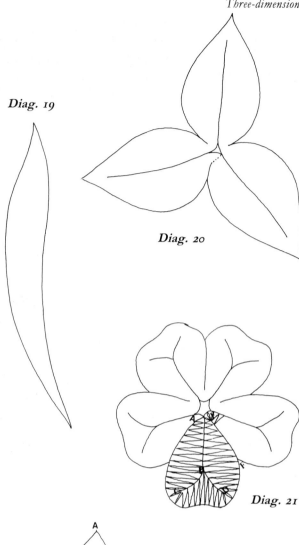

Diag. 19

Diag. 20

Diag. 21

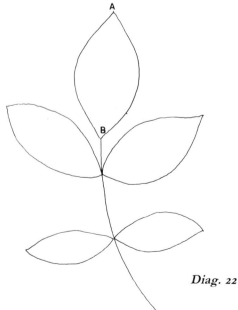

Diag. 22

Daffodil-type leaves

All this family have long, thin leaves, usually very veined (Diag. 19). They can therefore be worked with twists and/or different weights or colours of thread.

Begin at *A* with three pairs and increase on every row to nine pairs. Use wire as before. Bunch the threads at the bottom and tie off in a tassel. Make as many as necessary to make an artistic arrangement. The leaves are as important as the flowers.

Tulips

Follow the same procedure as the other flowers, using eight pairs plus wire and one other thread. Tulips and some other members of the lily family have overlapping petals wider at the base. Two groups of three petals from Diag. 20 allow for this. Half stitch one group and cloth stitch with veins the other. Assemble with wire stalk, stamens and a calyx to cover any threads. Three petals up and three down form an iris.

Dog rose

Rose petals are heart-shaped and can be worked in such a way that they have colour in the triangle formed at their top. Begin with *A* in Diag. 21 with four pairs plus wire and one other thread. Increase to 10 pairs and have a pale pink pair on the outer edge. Leave out a pair on every pin from *B* to *C*, turn on pin *C* and use the pink pair as the weaver. Take each pair in from *C* to *B* using the same pinholes and leave out on the pinholes *B* to *D*. Turn on pin *D* and change to white weaver, take in the left-out pairs from *D* to *B* using the same pinholes and sewing in from *B* to *A*. Turn on pin *E* but do not sew in from *E* to *F* – just use the same pinholes. Continue to work all the petals in this way. Half stitch can be used for the sides and cloth stitch for the centre tip. Fig. 12 shows the complete flower.

Double roses have several of these, all assembled together.

Rose leaves

Begin at *A* in Diag. 22 with three pairs and wire, and increase to twelve pairs as quickly as possible adding two pairs on each pin. Make a vein by twisting the weaver twice and work with a picot edge to *B*. Leave the threads and wire about four inches. Make four more leaves graduating in size.

Assembly

Attach some stamens to a doubled wire and push

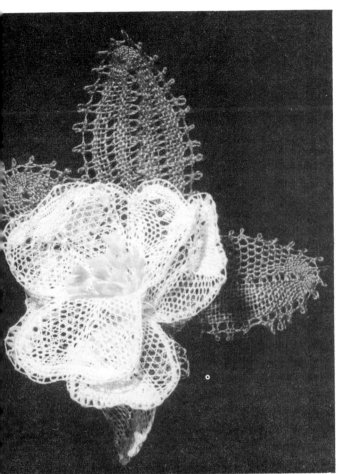

Fig. 12   *Wild rose*

Fig. 13   *Orchids*

through the petals and calyx; bind firmly. Bind the threads and wires from the top leaf and attach the others as shown. Attach the leaf to the flower.

Diag. 23

Orchid

Begin at *A* in Diag. 23 with four pairs and increase to eight pairs plus wire and one thread to form the pair. Work in cloth stitch adding twists to vary the texture. Change to half stitch and a picot edge for the second petal, sewing in down the centre of the petals but not where they join one another or where they join the lip. The petals need to be as free as possible for assembly. Decrease to four pairs at *B* and make a narrow braid with a picot edge to *A*. Sew out and tie off. Sew in pairs at the lower end of the lip and work the filling, sewing and tying out in the centre. Torchon ground and tallies have been marked but any filling can be substituted.

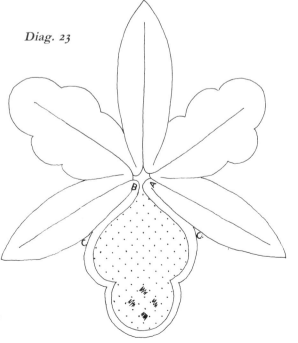

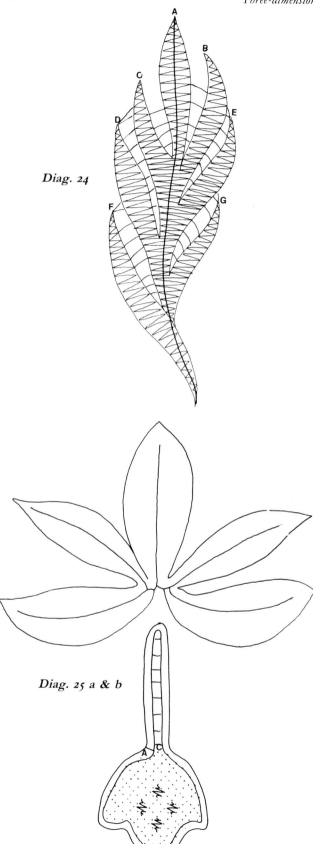

Diag. 24

Diag. 25 a & b

Assembly

Join BC to AC to form a cone. Join A to B under the cone so that the lip is pushed out and up. Attach stamens to a doubled wire and push this through the lip and the petals. Hold firmly and bind the stem as before. Make sure that the edge of the circle of petals is held by the tape to the stem.

Skeleton leaf or feather

This makes a very good base or background to daisies, chrysanthemums and the larger flowers. No wire is needed but it can be added as a vein at the back of the leaf afterwards – this makes the leaf more feathery in appearance.

Begin at A in Diag. 24 with three pairs and increase to 11 on each side at every row. Leave out pairs where shown for leaflets B and C. Start C with three pairs and increase to five, work down, take in pairs from A, and join to the centre three pairs where they meet, leaving pairs as indicated for D. Repeat on the other side B, joining to the centre when reached and leaving pairs out for E. Start D with two pairs and take in from C leaving out for F. Start E with the two pairs left out from B and leave out for G. These join to the centre as they meet. Work leaves G and F and finally collect all the threads in on leaf F decreasing to four pairs at the base. Tie off.

Orchid 2

The pattern was taken by pressing the flower parts and drawing round them. Cream and pale pink threads were used. The main petals (Diag. 25a) are worked in cloth stitch; the same eight pairs work throughout, close at the base and open out with twists as the petal widens. Wire is used as a gimp and the openness of the cloth gives it a very lacy appearance.

The trumpet is worked separately (see Diag. 25b), starting at A and finishing at A. Its filling is added afterwards from the base B, to sew out at the top C.

Assembly

Assemble by joining the petals and bending the trumpet to form an arc. Insert a bent stalk wire through the trumpet at C and through the centre of the petals. Sew if necessary. Cover the stalk with florists' tape.

Flowers in Buckinghamshire point

Do not attempt these until you have experience of Bucks rounds. This pattern (Diag. 26) is worked in the same way as Bucks rounds of six segments. Each

Fig. 14   *Single orchid*

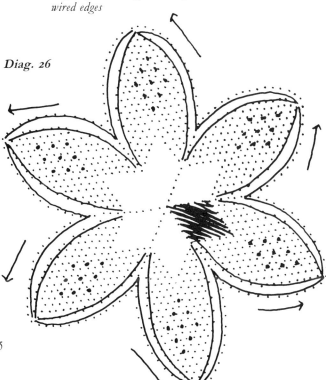

Fig. 15   *Buckinghamshire flowers with wired edges*

petal is worked in the direction indicated. Use wire on the outside edge and allow the pairs to increase in the very sharp indent. There will be about 14 pairs; pull these tight.

Assembly

Assemble with stamens through the centre as before and bind the inserted wire stalk with tape. The fillings within the petals can be varied to produce different effects. Fig. 15 shows the flowers complete.

Insects

Most insects can be worked in three dimensions but the most effective are those that have wings. Beetles, spiders and other crawling insects are very effective in embroidery, as a feature can be made of the patterning on the body; but they have nothing to attract a lace-

Diag. 26

maker. Given below are patterns for a simple butterfly which makes a feature of the spaces in the wing, and the realistic veining pattern on the wing; a Mayfly, which has a different shape of body and wings that are worked in one piece; and a ladybird, which has a fat body with solid top wings and lacy under wings. Other insects such as lace flies, dragonflies and bees fall into one or other of the techniques given.

All have double bodies, which eliminates the tuft when finishing off and covers the joinings of wings. The body can be lightly padded and small wire legs can be inserted.

Butterfly

Begin on the antennae with four pairs and work stem stitch to the head. Use these pairs to work the body down to the tip. Do not decrease but work the underside to the head and tie off the threads in pairs. Cut off leaving the threads 10 cm long.

Begin the wing at *A* in Diag. 27 sewing in four pairs and wire plus one thread as a pair. Work in twisted cloth stitch to *B*, add two pairs and plait them to *C*. Sew in two pairs at *D* and plait to *C*. Make a windmill crossing at *C* and continue plaiting to *E* and *F*. Divide the plait at *E* and twist each pair four times. Continue the wing to *G*. Leave the wire pair out and continue the braid taking in the twisted pairs at *H* and *I* and leaving them out at *J* and *K*. Plait these to *F*.

Make a windmill at *F* and sew out at *L* to cross the body for the opposite wing. Plait to *M* and take these

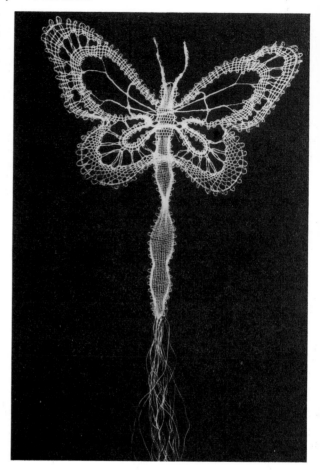

Fig. 16 *Butterfly showing the double body and crossing threads*

into the braid at *M*. Sew the braid in at the body at *N*, turn on a pin and sew out into the body to cross the body at *O*. Work on the other side to *P* in readiness for the continuation of the wire.

Sew in five pairs at *G* and with the wire pair included, work the outer wing, sewing into the inner as shown and making cloth stitch and twist to accommodate the changing width. Sew into the inner wing at *Q* and change to half stitch for the under wing. Sew in and cross the body at *R*, taking the wire across as well. Make the opposite outer wing, absorbing the pairs into the braid left at *P*. Continue the braid with the wire but tie out the threads from the outer wing. Sew in finally at *S*.

Assembly

While still attached to the pillow, fold up the under-body to cover the threads. Add a small amount of

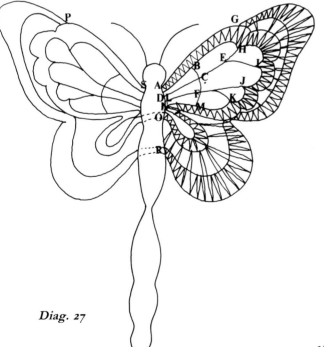

Diag. 27

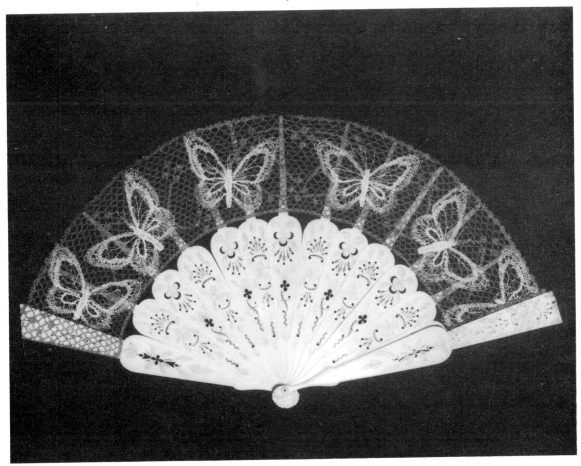

Fig. 17 *Butterflies used on a fan*

padding if desired but often the threads that have been left are enough. Sew the two parts of the body together and then remove from the pillow. The wings can be bent to the desired shape. If the butterfly is to be used as a brooch, a pin can be attached to the under-body. It is possible to have the wings in a different colour from the body, to have the outer wing different from the inner wing, and by changing the weaver for the under-body to incorporate a different colour here.

Mayfly

The main feature of the mayfly is the tail, so it is necessary to make both parts of the body separately and join them at the tail. Finish one 'body' but leave the threads long at the tail end. Make the other one and leave on the pillow with long tail threads. Tie out all but three pairs. Work the underwings first in half stitch with eight pairs and wire starting at *A* in Diag. 28 and sewing out at *B*. This wing can have surface leaves as illustrated. The threads can be left long to use as padding. Work the top wings with or without the gimp thread as veining. Begin at the tip *C* by laying the threads across as in Diag. 28 and working both sides simultaneously; add pairs as necessary to make the ground. Take the accumulation of threads out as the body is approached, and tie out.

Assembly

With the fly still on the pillow, lay the under-body on top. Pin down and tuck in all the loose threads leaving out three pairs from each body at the tip. Take one pair from each side and plait for the required length; tie off and cut.

Sew the lower body to the upper, and then take it off the pillow. The mayfly works very well in metallic threads and will not need any wire.

27

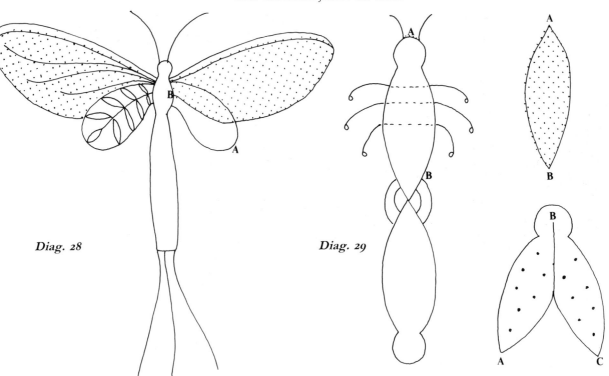

Diag. 28

Diag. 29

Ladybird

Begin with the antennae as in the butterfly and add four more pairs at *A* in Diag. 29. A thicker pair on the outside of the body helps to hold the shape. Add this by weaving it through the threads before starting and using it as a pair with a thin thread on each side (as with a Honiton coarse thread).

Leave out pairs on each side from *B* to the tip and take them in again on the lower body as indicated. This enables one to have a pointed body. Leave long ends at the head end, tie and cut off.

Underwings

Start at *A* with wire and three pairs. Increase and decrease as necessary to make the ground to *B*. Bunch the threads at the base *B*.

Outer wings

Begin at *A* with three pairs (no wire) and increase to 14 pairs. Work cloth stitch with raised tallies for the spots, turn on pin *B* and work to the wing tip, sewing in from *B* to *C* and decreasing to three pairs at *D*. Tie these and weave them back down the wing.

Diag. 30

Assembly

Fig. 18 shows the successive stages. Cover three 10 cm lengths of wire with thread for the legs and insert them across the body. Pad and sew the under-body to the upper, tucking in the loose threads from the head and tail. Place the under-wings into position and attach the top wings at the head end.

Bee

Make the body (Diag. 30) in the same way as the ladybird but use a fluffy thread as an occasional weaver to create stripes. Make half stitch wings in a very fine thread.

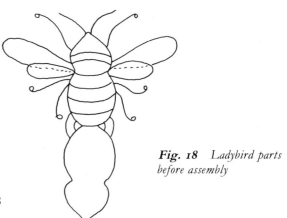

Fig. 18 *Ladybird parts before assembly*

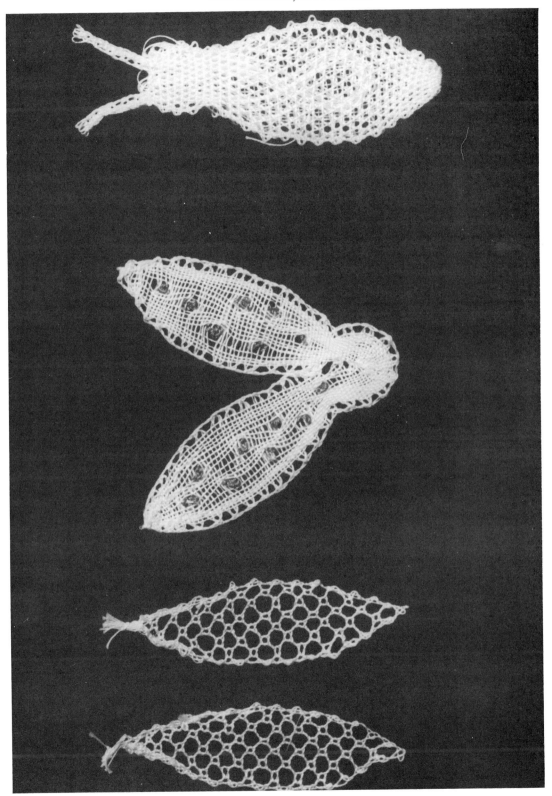

THREE

The use of lace stitches

The intricate structures of stitches that make up bobbin lace are the most exciting part of lacemaking; it is quite easy, especially when using colour, to forget that these stitches are the very thing that gives lace its beauty. There is a very close relationship with weaving; and it is tempting to make cloth stitch areas too dense, when there should be a delicate 'see-through' quality. This quality is worth some very careful thought when mounting lace.

The choice of these stitches is very wide, sometimes too wide (see *The Book of Bobbin Lace Stitches* by Bridget M. Cook and Geraldine Stott; published by Batsford) but it is possible to divide them into categories when designing for different purposes and effects.

Those with a distinct linear quality can be used in buildings, dresses and landscapes:

Twisted cloth	Cucumber
Cane ground	Fish
Bias ground	Some spider stitches
Some rose grounds	Ribbon
Half stitch diamond	Some bud and star grounds

Those with an all-over pattern can be used as backgrounds where no distinct line or pattern is desirable. These divide into light, medium and dense, as follows:

Light	*Medium*	*Dense*
Torchon	Cobweb	Half stitch
Bucks point	Kat stitch	The Armures
Honeycomb	Garter stitch	Herringbone
Mechlin	Feather	Toad in the hole
Valenciennes	Blossom	Italian spider
	Braid and	Spider and tallies
	winkie pins	Haloed spider
	Tallies and	Birdcage
	lattice	Bud star
		Toile star
		Shell star

Some have a distinct pattern or shape, and are suitable for trees, buildings, or dresses, and where a bold pattern is required:

Gauze shapes	Pin filling
Triangular	Cushion
Whole stitch blocks	Devon no pin
Rose ground	Point d'esprit
Mayflower	Marguerites
Zeccatello	Maltese leaves
Flags	Pheasant's eye
Clover	Haloed spider
Braided leaves	Bud star
Moulinet	Toile star
Blossom	Shell star
Wall	Pea
Brick	

Some of these fall into the all-over category when a dense bold area is required.

There are also those which can be drawn in by eye to fit an unusual shape. Most of the plaited grounds and some of the distinct shapes can be used such as spiders, peas, fish, feather and Maltese leaves.

A plaited ground can change with Maltese leaves to represent flowers, and with cloth stitch or half stitch to suggest leaves as in Fig. 19 and Diag. 31. This idea has been used in the 'Girl and the Peacocks' and in the 'Girl with the Horse'. The technique is very useful when putting in a complete background of lace stitches but some care is needed in the calculation of threads and their positions.

These grounds need not rely on graph paper but can be worked out by eye. They can then lose any linear look and by careful calculation can be made to follow a drawing. Very few pictures have strong, straight lines and for a feeling of movement it is essential to have curved ones. One of the difficulties is

Fig. 19 *Flowers by Eeva Lisa Kortalahti*

Diag. 31

planning the lines of these threads so that they can come in and out of a foot side, without the need to add pairs on one side and take out on the other. Diagonal grounds come out on one side and in and out on the other as in Diag. 32, so they can be drawn at any angle to allow for this. Those that lie straight can have grounds which start at one side and go back in the reverse direction. Not every ground will do this but a few will: half stitch, half stitch torchon, garter stitch, twisted half stitch ground, honeycomb, Brussels net – any others will need an experimental sample first.

Simple scenes using a variety of stitches can be interesting on their own, but other features may be added, such as houses, people etc.

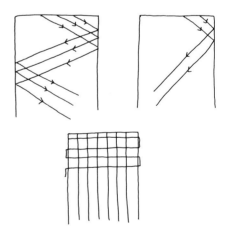

Diag. 32

Basic scene

This illustrates the change from plait to leaf within a ground with a base in other stitches (Diag. 33 and Fig. 20).

Make the outer tape frame first with six pairs. Work each section of the hills in order *A, B, C, D*. These can be in cloth stitch and half stitch as shown or, if the whole picture is enlarged, in other filling stitches.

Remember that the further away the hills are the more open in texture they should be. The base parts are worked from right to left or left to right and the sky and leaves are worked last from top to bottom following the arrows.

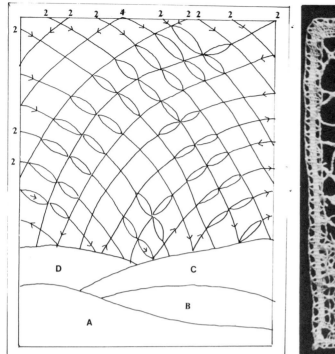

Diag. 33

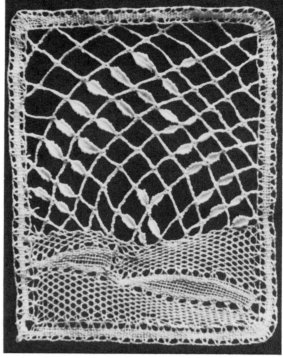

Fig. 20   *Scene using plaits and Maltese leaves*

Fig. 21   *Tree worked in Torchon ground and Maltese leaves*

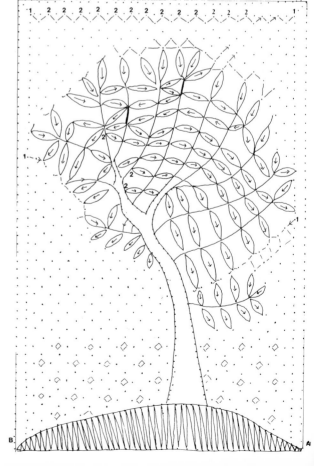

Diag. 34

Scene with tree

This is worked from top to bottom (Diag. 34) using all the threads to proceed down the picture, changing from torchon net to leaves where shown and back again to ground, sewing in and tying off in the half stitch base.

Work the frame as before starting at *B*; at *A* change to half stitch and add six more pairs to make a firm base. Finish at *B* with three pairs and tie off. Sew in pairs as shown at the top and work the tree; add pairs where shown to make sure that there are enough pairs for a firm tree trunk. The heavier line indicates a thicker plait to carry the threads along. Pairs go out of the tree to the top right-hand side and come in again as shown by the arrows.

The complete scene is shown in Fig. 21. The torchon ground can change to a variety of rose grounds before tying out into the half stitch hill.

Tree in a landscape

This is a more complicated pattern (Fig. 22) and is best worked after the previous one.

Make a frame as before with six pairs and sew in pairs at the top (58 pairs). Work the sky and the tree as before. Leave the pairs hanging when they reach the hills but continue the tree trunk to *A* in Diag. 35 and tie these pairs; leave them about 20 cm long, and cut off. Work *B* from right to left in bias ground, sewing in pairs at the tree and using the pairs that have been left out from the sky. Keep a foot side on the edges, add pairs where necessary and sew out into the frame.

Work *C* from left to right, making the leaves first and half stitch over the top for the bush and a half stitch hedge. Some pairs can be left out for the mayflower ground at *D*. Work *D*. Work *E* in a rose ground from left to right taking the threads across the tree trunk and sewing out into *C*. Some of these threads can be left out for *F* in bias ground from left to right, taking in pairs from the sky. Work *G* in mayflower from right to left, crossing the tree and sewing in to *B* and *E*.

Work *H* from right to left, sewing into *G* and taking the tied tree-trunk threads through to tie off over the ground. Figs. 22 and 23 show the Flanders ground which is very dense but other grounds of equal density can be used. Work *I* from left to right and *J* from side to side sewing into *I* and *H* to sew out all the threads in finally at the base of the frame.

Fig. 22 *Tree scene using a variety of stitches for the hills*

Fig. 23 *Tree scene on a fan with stitches used for the tree shapes*

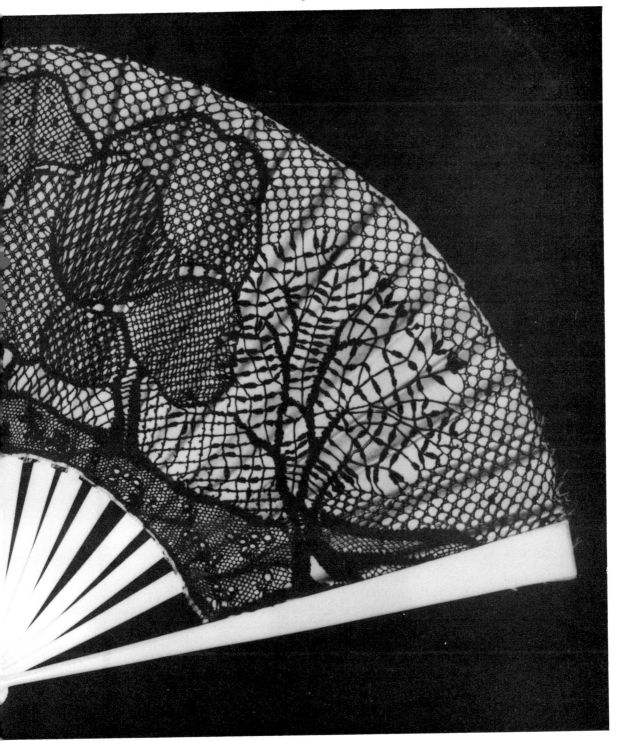

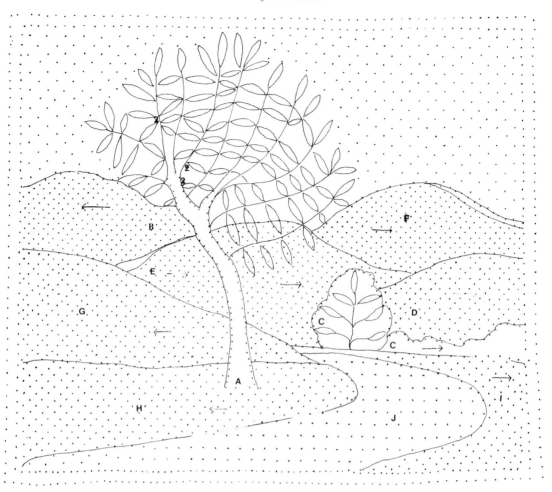

Diag. 35

The four seasons

The next four scenes represent the seasons; designed by Annemarie Rager of Belgium, they are drawings with a hint to the fillings and are open to individual interpretation: Diags. 36–9 and Figs. 24–5.

There is a point where tape lace, Honiton lace and Bruges lace meet and overlap. In all three, sewings are needed for joining and for putting in fillings to the open areas. The difference comes in that unlike tape lace, Honiton and Bruges have extra pairs added and subtracted as required. Bruges lace carries the threads over the work more than in Honiton, but this is because the thread is coarser and therefore shows more. With this technique the structure of each design must be worked out in advance. Honiton is a very fine

lace and the sewings out and removal each time do not show, but it is certainly quicker to carry the threads along and this technique was probably more of a feature in Bruges where speed was essential to the lace industry. Samples of antique Honiton (Fig. 26) often show that this was also done at the time when Honiton was an industry in England. If a coarser thread is used for these techniques it is better to carry the threads along as much as the design will allow. The essential stages therefore are the design and the

Fig. 24 *A scene using textured threads and soft colours; by Annemarie Rager*

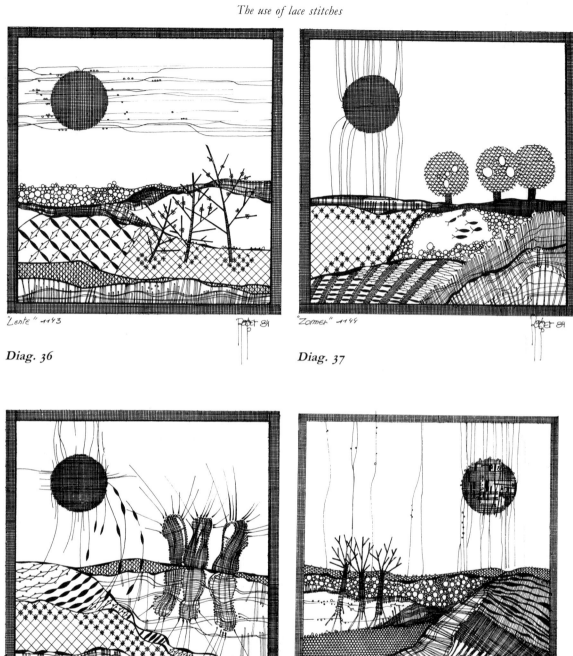

"Lente" 1143   Rager 84

Diag. 36

"Zomer" 1144   Rager 84

Diag. 37

"Herfst" 1145   Rager 84

Diag. 38

Winter   Rager 84

Diag. 39

Fig. 25 *A scene using textured threads and superimposed reeds; by Annemarie Rager*

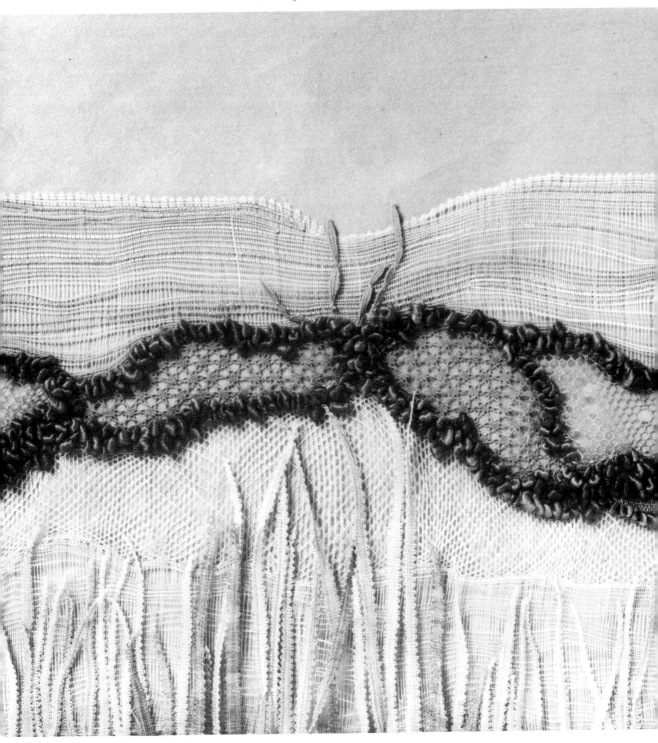

order of work. The planning of the work is as important as the working of it; the more organized the drawing, the easier it is to produce a good piece of work. An old saying was always: 'Your lace is as good as your pricking'; many of the old prickings did not produce good lace probably because they deteriorated with constant use, and the workers did not have the skill to reprick them correctly.

Sunflower inset

The small braid on the inside of the flower is worked first in stem stitch with the foot on the outside. Start at

Fig. 26 *Antique Honiton showing the threads carried over the work in a continuous way so that there is no tying off until the end*

Diag. 40

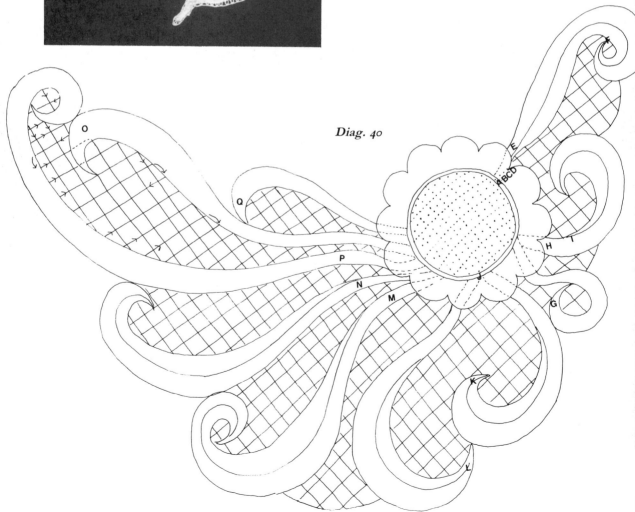

A and sew out at *A* (Diag. 40). Five pairs. Use these threads to begin the petals, adding two pairs at *B*, *C*, and *D*. Put in a coarse pair as in Honiton and add two more pairs on the outer curve so that there are 13 pairs in all. Work the petals in half stitch, taking the coarse pair across as in Honiton to indent the petals. Join with sewings at *A*, *B*, *C* and *D*, tie but do not cut off, and use these to start *E*. Add more pairs as required. Turn at *F* and half stitch back to *E*. Sew out and cut off. Work from tip *G* to the flower, sewing in to the inner braid and across the petals so that they can stand up diagonally. Do not sew into the petals – these lie free. Turn at the inner braid and use the same pairs for *H*, turning at the tip and half stitch to *I*. Sew out. Begin the next leaves at *J* turning them at *K* and *L* to half stitch and sew out. Work *M* and *N* in a similar way. *O* starts at the tip, sews into the inner braid and

out again for *P*. *Q* is worked from its tip to sew out in the inner braid.

Work the spider filling in the flower centre with a finer thread, sewing into the stem stitch with top sewings (as in Honiton lace) so that the stem stitch forms a raised edge.

The ground that holds the leaves together, which is necessary if the lace is being used in a neckline, is worked with a coarser thread and is carried over the work as much as possible. As it travels from left to right and from right to left, it is essential to choose a ground which will do this.

Fig. 27 shows the complete sunflower inset.

Fig. 27 *Sunflower dress inset*

Lampshade petal (make six)

These when assembled (Figs 28–9; Diag. 41) make a shade for an Art Nouveau lamp but if reduced in size will make a flower that could be used as a table centre. Begin at *A* with four pairs and increase to ten pairs with a wire as a gimp or coarse pair on the outer edge only. Turn and cross at *B* and change to half stitch. Turn with sewings at *C* and change to cloth stitch at *D*; sew out at *E*. The wire can be taken all the way round but can also be left out when travelling up the middle section if desired. Add the fillings by sewing in pairs as required and work any ground. A Mayflower filling has been marked but you can make your own choice. Work a zigzag plait in the centre.

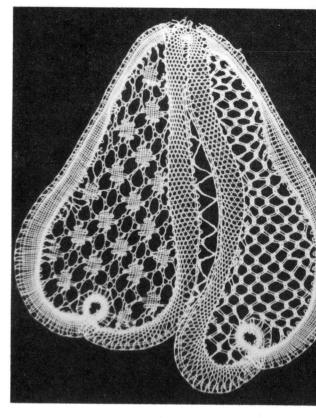

Fig. 28 *Petal from an Art Nouveau lamp in tape lace with fillings*

Diag. 41

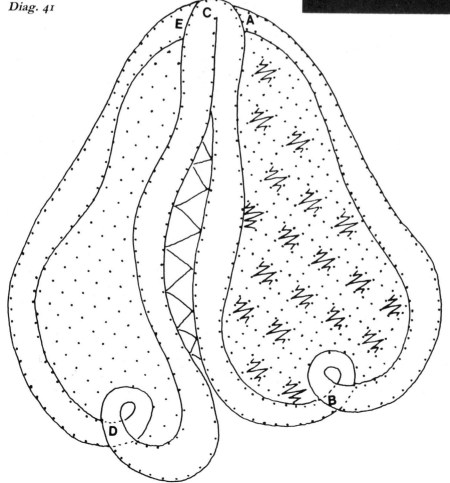

Butterfly inset

This inset (Fig. 30) is designed to fit a neckline or a corner and can be reduced or enlarged.

Begin at the antennae (Diag. 42) and work stem stitch from *A* to the head on each side; use these pairs to work the body and tie off at the tip *B*. Sew pairs into the body at *C* and work the under-wing, turning at *D* and changing to half stitch. Cross the body at *C* and work the other side.

Begin the upper wing at *E*, sew into the body and out for *F*, turn at *G*, and change to half stitch to sew out at *H*. Work *I* to *K* turning at *J*, and cross the body to work the other side. Finish the other wing and add any filling to the spaces.

The coloured butterfly fan was worked in this way but with more scrolls.

Fig. 29   *Art Nouveau lamp*

Fig. 30   *Butterfly inset in cream and gold threads*

43

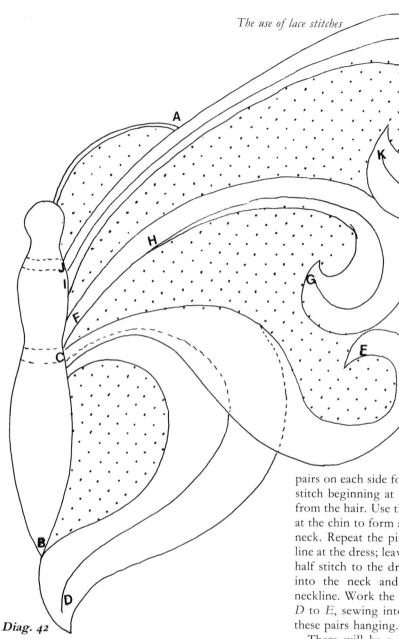

Fig. 31 *Dancing girl
adapted from a painting*

Diag. 42

Dancing girl

This is an example (Fig. 31) of carrying threads over as much as possible and putting in a background rather than a filling.

Work the frame first and then push the pins down. Start the arm at *A* in Diag. 43 and work in cloth stitch to *B*; leave these threads hanging (eight pairs). Begin at the top of the head with three pairs; add on each side to 12 pairs. Work in twisted cloth, dividing at the face and working the hair on both sides, dropping out

pairs on each side for the face. Work the face in cloth stitch beginning at the top and bringing in the pairs from the hair. Use the same pin holes again. Pin pairs at the chin to form a dividing line and then work the neck. Repeat the pinning of pairs to form the break line at the dress; leave these pairs hanging. Work *C* in half stitch to the dress break, using six pairs sewing into the neck and reducing to two pairs at the neckline. Work the second sleeve with six pairs from *D* to *E*, sewing into the neck and to the arm; leave these pairs hanging.

There will be a lot of pairs hanging at different points but they now all come together to make the dress, eliminating sewings and cut-off threads. Work the bodice using the threads from the neck and taking in the pairs from the first sleeve. Sew into the arm and take the threads across to sew in on the other side. Start the bodice again with the threads from *E*, taking in the threads from the upper bodice as they are reached. Leave three pairs at *F* and two pairs at each pin to *G*. Begin the skirt at *F*; take pairs in from the bodice and drop pairs out for the next skirt panel. Take in the pairs from *B* to *Q* but leave out four pairs again at *O*. Work each panel of the dress using the

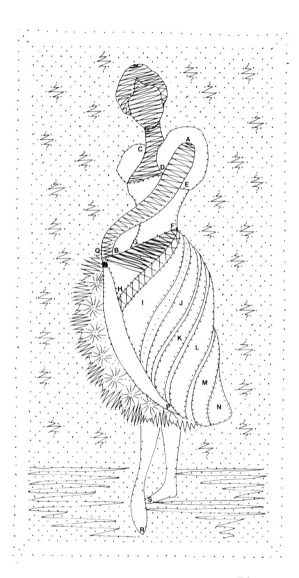

Diag. 43

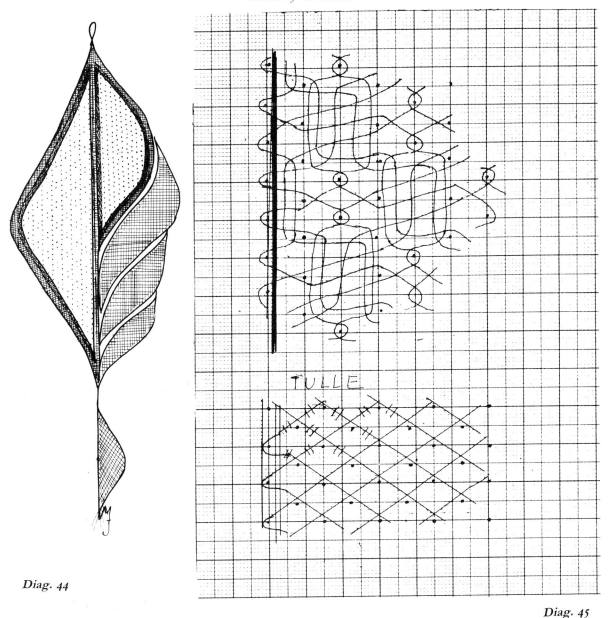

Diag. 44

pairs from the panel before and adding one extra pair to start the panel where necessary. Diminish the pairs as they accumulate in panels *M* and *N*, and finish off. Work *O* to *P* with the four pairs at *O*, adding another two pairs and sewing out at *P*. Work a fan and spider edge from *Q*, starting with three pairs and adding as necessary. Sew out into the skirt. Work both legs in cloth stitch from edge at *P* down to *R* and *S*, taking them over the lace edge. Threads from *S* can be absorbed into leg *R*; finish with minimal pairs at *R*.

Work the honeycomb ground from the frame top, sewing into the figure tying out or using again. Work cloth stitch shading at the base. This figure, if reduced, can be worked in Honiton using Honiton methods.

Abstract motif

The motif in Diag. 44, designed by Marie Jeanne Cooreman, has a raised edge round the fillings and worked in cloth stitch and half stitch. The fillings are Fond de Neige and Tulle as in Diag. 45.

47

FOUR

Rounds

Graph papers for regular one-piece laces

We use graph paper for lace design because of the geometrical structure of one-piece laces. Threads have to travel across as in weaving, or diagonally as in lace grounds, in order for the piece to hold together as a piece of material with continuous threads. The usual method is to use graph papers of different gauges to suit the size of thread and of different angles to give a changing shape of ground. Ninety degrees gives an angular ground suitable for Torchon; 60° is used commonly for Point ground, but its diamond shape is often too pointed for floral designs and therefore 52° is considered a better angle for this purpose.

These papers are very suitable for straight edges but when a continuous shape of a different kind is required, it is worthwhile exploring different graph papers.

Circular graph paper or polargraph paper has many uses. Circular shapes are very pleasing to the eye and parts of a circle are the basis for fans, collars, cone lampshades etc. Designing ground laces to fit these shapes has always been difficult when using a graph paper based on straight lines. The principle of polargraph paper is that the ground lines when plotted on the paper form arcs and there is no change of direction as the circle is worked. The main problem is that the ground reduces in size as you approach the centre (Diag. 46), and so you cannot work from a complete circle to a centre in point ground in this way; however, the method can be used successfully for circular edges. It also produces a change in angle from top to bottom, as can be seen in the segment shown in Diag. 46. This does not seem to alter the laces' appearance and is often useful in design.

Polargraph paper can be marked out in ways that will produce a ground for Torchon collars, one way for coarse point ground and one for fine point.

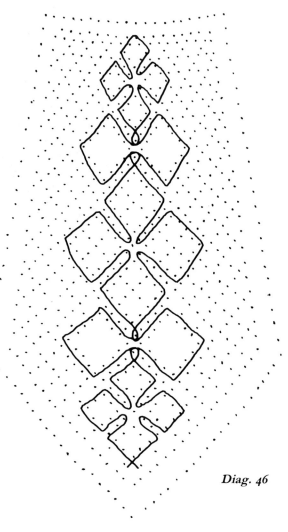

Diag. 46

Polargraph paper without the dots is useful for Bedfordshire rounds.

Bedfordshire circle 1

This is designed with very little deviation from the basic round graph; the concentric circles and the radii (Fig. 32) are the ground lines. As indicated by the arrows in Diag. 47, the lines travel from the outer edge to the inner circle and back on each row. Double blossom was used for the panels between the flowers and two colours, green and white, were used quite successfully by hanging a pair of white and a pair of green at the flower petals, using the white as the weaver and then allowing the pairs to carry on throughout.

This ring can be buttonholed to a metal ring to use as a window mobile or in the base of a lamp. Enlarge the pattern if necessary to fit ring size.

Bedfordshire circle 2

This is a little more complicated (Diag. 48) and can be worked in several colours (see colour photographs). The following are some suggestions:

Two pairs brown for the shell edge weavers
Seven pairs cream for the triangle

Fig. 32 *Bedfordshire circle attached to a lampshade ring for insertion in the base of a drum lampshade*

One pair yellow and one pair brown for outer flowers
Five pairs pale green for the trail, the stalk which goes in and out to the next trail
Eight pairs in shades of green (graduated colours) for the leaves
Four pairs green or brown for the inner trail
Two pairs rust for the centre petals
Three pairs yellow for the centre trail.

Work as indicated by the arrows.

Designing ground laces

Torchon collar

The most difficult part of the design for a torchon collar is its front edges. To start, one works the triangle *ABC* in the direction indicated in Diag. 49. All the pairs will now be hanging from *B* to *C*. The pillow turns as when turning a corner, and work proceeds as for a straight edge until the other end when the pairs finish as the work is turned again. This collar blank has been left for you to work out a design within its shell edge: spiders, diamonds, trails, gimp threads or a collar of one fancy ground only – the choice is yours.

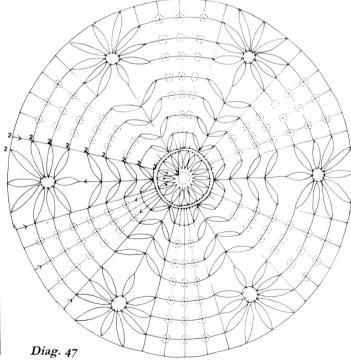

Diag. 47

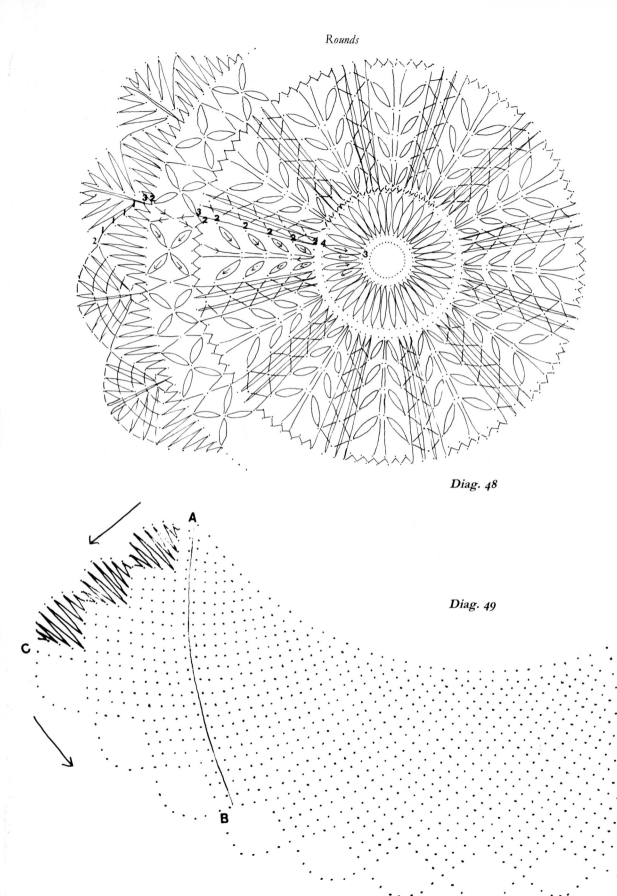

Diag. 48

Diag. 49

Fig. 33 *Buckinghamshire fan worked on circular graph paper*

Circles in point ground

To design a circular form as an edge, it is perhaps easier to use a traditional shape from an old pricking. This will work well and after adaptation a new design will form without the need for drawing ability. Merely by adding a line here and there, one can impose one's own individuality, and this can lead to new designing. Draw out the circle required on to tracing paper and arrange the shapes (Diag. 50) round the edge. Arrange them the same distance apart to fit as a repeat. Do not worry about having spaces in between as this is where one can place new ideas. A motif can be repeated but spaced as in Diag. 51, or a motif, or group of motifs, can be reversed so that a different pattern forms.

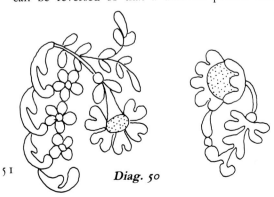

Diag. 50

51

Diag. 51

When satisfied with the result in rough, draw in the pattern, gimp line only. Make sure that the edge lies accurately on the circle edge. You will then draw in other leaves to fill the space and within the circle, and any remaining areas created can have a different stitch. When the design is satisfactory (Fig. 33), place the tracing on to the prepared graph paper matching inner and outer curves to the concentric circles on the graph. Mark in the grounds and the fillings first, followed by the dots in the cloth areas; mark in the picot edge and work either on the tracing, or on a photocopy of it, or prick on to card. It is only necessary to work out one section fully – a photocopier can save a lot of work by repeating the section and, if required, reducing or enlarging it.

To work the circular edge use segment *ABCD* and begin on the heavy line marked, so as not to show the final join.

To make this pattern into a fan or dress yoke reverse the segment and extend the depth to *E*.

To make a pleasing design however a pattern is needed at the inner and side edges. This can be achieved by using again a traditional small edge and arranging it in the same way on the inner circle. The side edges need only be simple shapes or honeycomb holes. The edge that is already drawn needs extending to *A* in Diag. 51.

To work a fan, start at *A* and work the side edge and the outer edge simultaneously, adding pairs where necessary. Follow the ground lines which are arcs (*E* to *F*) from side edge to outer until the ground lines are established. You finish as you began: take out pairs as they accumulate. A fan always has part of the lace obscured by one stick and the other one visible. It is therefore convenient that the start edge is visible and the finish edge is obscured.

Peter Pan collars

These collars in one or two pieces are an extension of the circular edge theme. They consist of either a complete circle or more often three quarters. This can be worked out by fitting a cut paper shape round the neck and trimming to fit the desired size.

The essential part of a collar is its front edges which are identical and very visible. It is necessary to reverse the pattern at centre back to achieve this.

Collar 1

This has a simple repeat which is turned at the front edge and has a half repeat at centre back. Plan in the same way as the circular edge, spacing the motifs (Diag. 52). The centre back is planned first and the

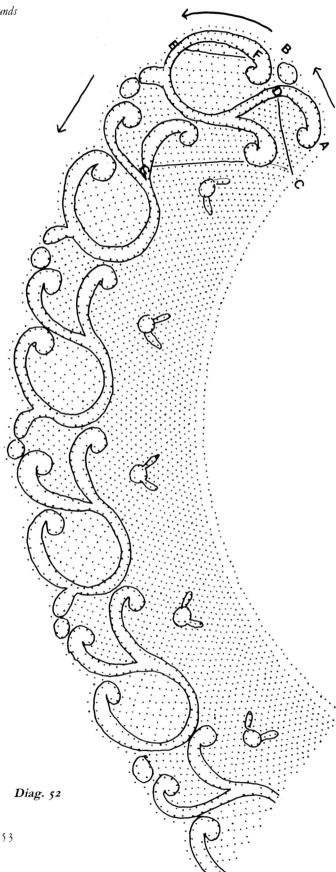

Diag. 52

edge is very visible and must be as neat as the other one.

The other alternative is to start the collar each time at centre front and make a neat join at centre back.

Collar 2

This was designed in the same way, spacing a motif, but a continuous edge in scallops added. The section *EFGH* in Diag. 53 is repeated again to centre back

Diag. 53

Fig. 34   Buckinghamshire collar

motifs spaced out to the centre front. This often involves some trial and error; traditional patterns can be accommodated quite well.

A design evolves; in the process, small rounds in either cloth or honeycomb are needed to link the motifs and to enable the gimp to follow through. Point net is too plain for the purpose, so either make a spotted net with tallies or introduce a small gimped motif at intervals. To work a collar designed in this way, the direction of the ground is all-important.

Referring to Diag. 52, begin at *A*; establish *A* to *B* in the direction indicated, and establish ground line *C* to *D*. Turn the pillow gradually and work from *B* to *E*; establish ground line *E* to *F*. Continue to work the collar ground in diagonal rows parallel to *E F* until *C* to *G*. Working will then be as any normal edge until the finishing, which follows the same routine in reverse. This finish needs a great deal of care as this

and then reversed for the other half. The continuous edge starts with the two trails at *A*; the outer is a half stitch with picots and the inner in cloth which accommodates the incoming and outgoing threads of the ground.

As in Collar 1, establish ground line *BC*, and turning the pillow gradually, work the trails down to establish *CD*. Continue to work the ground parallel to *CD*. Finish off in reverse. Fig. 34 shows the worked Collar 2.

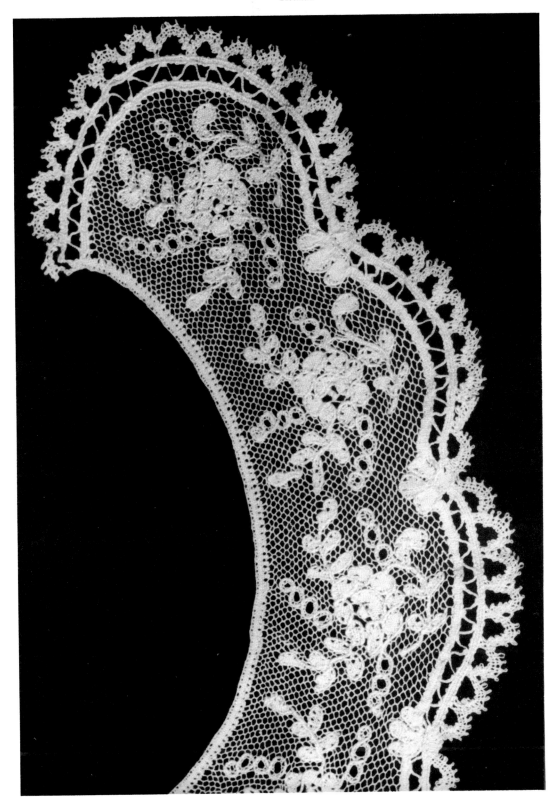

The Floral Dance

This consists of two circular edges joined with plaited bars (Fig. 35). The grounds used are point and honeycomb with the dresses worked in a variety of stitches. It can be worked just as successfully with Torchon stitches. The design has evolved from cut paper figures as in Diag. 54, with the trouser shape marked in. These shapes were then positioned on circular paper and the figures further divided into workable parts with suitable stitches marked (Diag. 55). By using brown weavers for the boy's suit and pink weavers for the girl's dress, it is possible to create a coloured effect. The whole pattern *ABCD* is reversed for each repeat, and 12 repeats form the circle. Each dress can be made different and more interesting by using different arrangements and stitches. The one shown is in rose ground. Start with

Fig. 35 The Floral Dance *with many fillings used for the dresses*

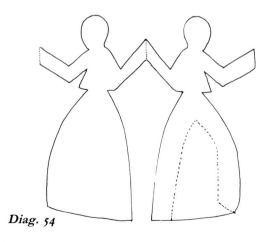

Diag. 54

Diag. 55

two pairs on each pin from *A* to *B* and introduce coloured weavers if and when required for sleeve, bodice, trousers or dress. It will be necessary to add extra pairs to keep the cloth firm as one does in floral Bucks, taking them out when not needed or carrying them with the gimp thread that surrounds the figures. The solid parts are in cloth or half stitch and the hair in cloth and twist.

The Town

The sections of the pattern join to form a circular town; the buildings are in cloth stitch with half stitch doors, and cloth and twist for some of the roofs. Some window openings have different stitches, and trees are in half stitch, or Maltese leaves as in Fig. oo. The pattern is worked with a surrounding gimp and extra pairs are added, as in floral Bucks, to make it solid.

The Town Hall

Start with the centre of the building (*C* to *D* in Diag. 56) as this makes a suitable place to join the work at the finish. Tallies are worked between the pillars and pairs of weavers meet at the roof, so that roof and main part are worked simultaneously. The clock is a spider.

The detached house

EFGH in Diag. 57 is again worked in cloth stitch, changing to half stitch for the door and with window openings having leaves for curtains and some crossed plaits for glazing bars. The fence throughout is formed by cloth stitch surrounded by a gimp which follows through at the bottom to form a continuous line.

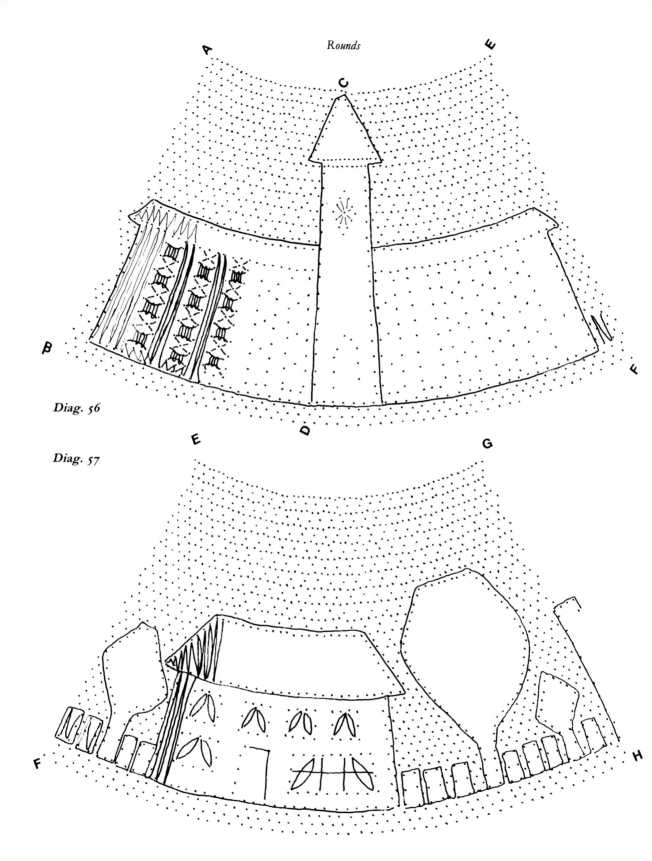

Diag. 56

Diag. 57

The church

GHIJ in Diag. 58 has castellations and the central tower has three sections with weavers meeting on alternate rows. The door is worked by dropping pairs out of the main structure and using these to form a cloth stitch door with twists to form a division. The window spaces are filled with crossed plaits and the clock is a spider.

The tall house is worked as the detached house but has rose ground windows.

The school or shops

IJKL in Diag. 59 has a central door worked as the church and the large windows are in torchon or point ground with gimped honeycombs.

The cottages

KLAB in Diag. 60 are worked as for all the houses with half stitch doors and plaited bars or crossed threads at the windows.

All these buildings can be freely interpreted and one need not follow the pattern exactly – there are numerous ways of using stitches to give different effects.

Diag. 58

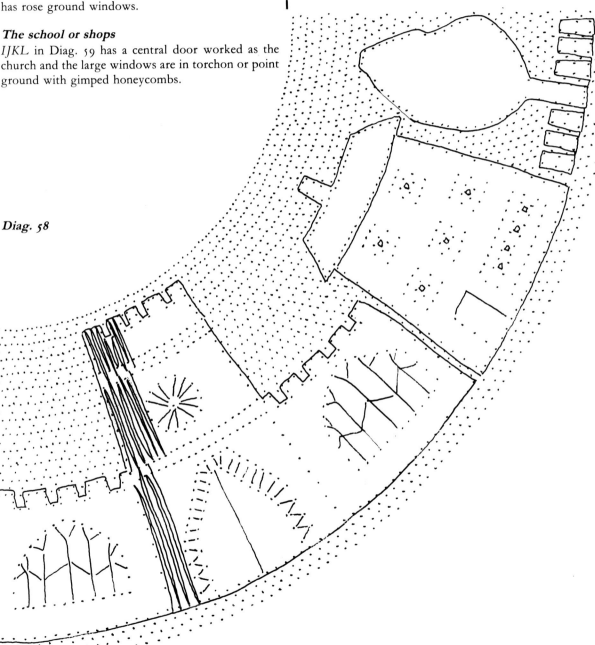

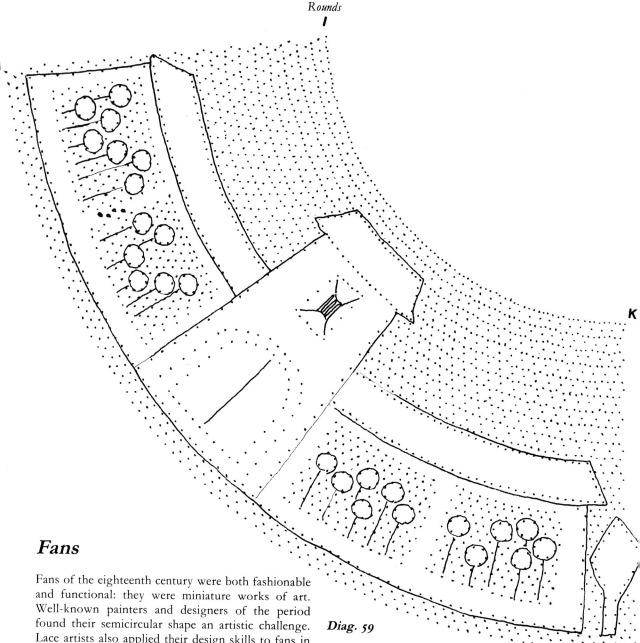

Diag. 59

Fans

Fans of the eighteenth century were both fashionable
and functional: they were miniature works of art.
Well-known painters and designers of the period
found their semicircular shape an artistic challenge.
Lace artists also applied their design skills to fans in
Chantilly and Point de Gaze, often combined with
painting to superb effect. Such fans were always very
expensive because the work was not repeated in
commercial quantities.

Many lacemakers are again making fans because of
their intricacy and aesthetic quality, and the challenge
of the shape. Lace is at its best when it has a certain
transparency and a fan is an ideal way to achieve this,
supported as it is only by sticks. The traditional lace
leaves were of the fine intricate laces of Valenciennes,
Chantilly, Bucks point, Honiton, Duchesse etc. –

60

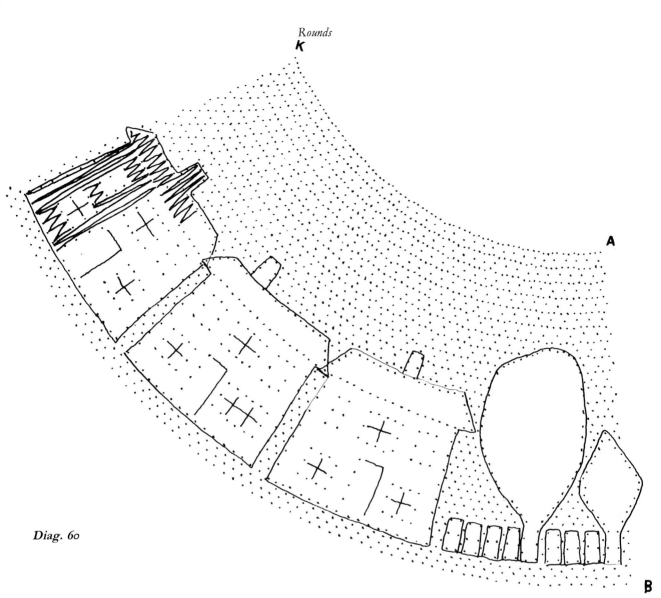

K

A

B

Diag. 60

never in Torchon which was regarded as a peasant lace and not appropriate to fan production. We however are at liberty to make a fan in any lace we choose.

Fans are half circles or slightly less, sometimes quarter circles and occasionally elliptical. The good lace fan must have the lace custom-made to fit the sticks; if the design on the lace matches the sticks so much the better. It is important to have the sticks to hand before designing the lace, although a few makers of sticks will make them to fit the lace. Because lace is delicate and decorative and takes time and skill, it is worthy of beautiful sticks. Wood is often too heavy and does not complement the lace in any way. Some antique lace fans are found with ebony sticks but more usual materials are bone, ivory, mother of pearl or tortoiseshell. Old fans can still be found, often with

damaged leaves in bric-à-brac shops. These are not usually sought after by collectors. Badly broken sticks are not worth buying but if the guards are in good condition it is possible to repair or remove the inner ones.

Cleaning and mending

Never wash sticks. Bone absorbs water and discolours; wood and tortoiseshell can warp; and mother of pearl falls apart as the glue dissolves. Some silicon cleaner polishes do the job well. Use a soft cloth and take great care as old sticks are usually very brittle and break easily. Use one of the instant adhesives to repair broken parts. If a stick is badly fractured it may be necessary to remove it, stick it to the adjacent one, or glue and reinforce it with a sliver of bone.

Fan design

Design in fans has always been very varied, and books on fans give many ideas that can be adapted. Pictorial fans were usually planned as a picture, others had scenes in three areas with patterning in between and yet others had an all-over pattern which followed the circular line. There are therefore many ways in which to organize the lace, including:

1. A wide edge at the top; a narrower edge at the bottom; ground in between worked in one piece. See Fig. 33.

2. A wide edge at the top; a narrow one at the bottom; an inset in between. Worked as three separate edges joined with sewings.

3. A complete scene worked as a picture but within a semicircle. See Fig. 23.

Fig. 36 *Torchon elliptical fan worked in black, gold and red with bead insertions. The design came from firework patterns*

Fig. 37 (opposite, top) *Bucks fan worked in cream silk in gold*

Fig. 38 (opposite, bottom) *Figures worked in petit point on silk canvas, surrounded with silk lace in honeycomb and point ground. The lace is pin stitched to the canvas*

4. An all-over geometric pattern. See Fig. 36.

5. Three or five shapes with patterning in between; can be floral Bucks or Honiton. See Fig. 37.

6. Small paintings or embroideries with a lace surround. See Fig. 38.

7. A stylized motif, e.g. butterfly, peacock, or bird, represented over a whole fan.

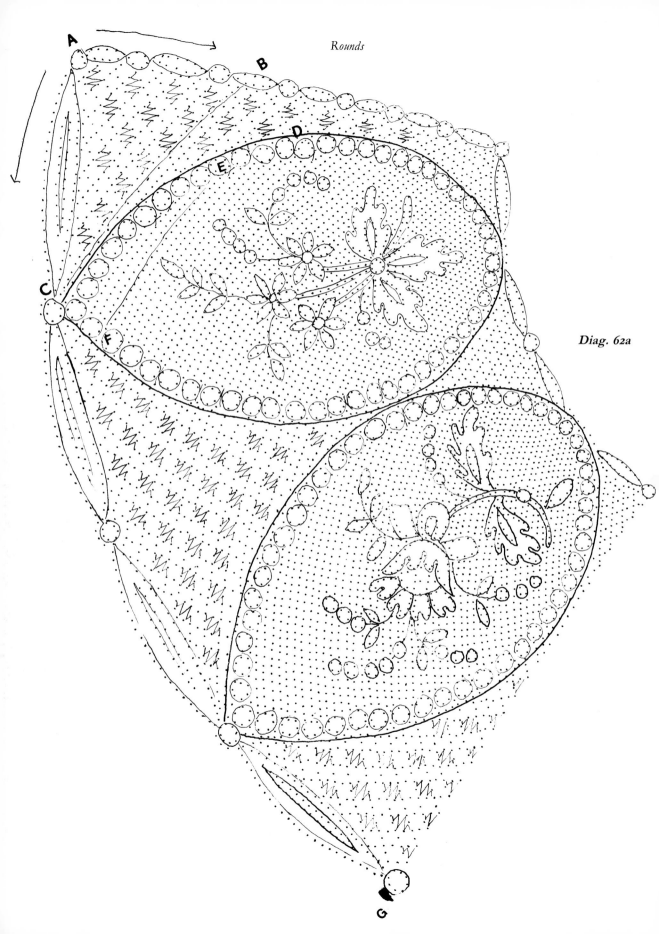

Rounds

Diag. 62a

The approach depends on the lacemaker's capabilities and the type of lace required. The first type has already been described, and is worked as a circular edge. It can be designed for Torchon, Bucks, Bedfordshire or any one-piece lace technique.

Preparation

To prepare the shape that the fan must take is simple. Sticks come in many different sizes and the shape must be made to fit what you have. Spread the sticks out to form the semicircle (Diag. 61) as evenly as possible on tracing paper. Draw in the inner circle and the outer circle, remove the sticks and place the tracing on to polargraph paper. Check the circle line with the graph paper and mark its position. Work out the design as in Diag. 62a, return the design to the graph, and mark in the dots. The following two fan patterns are in floral Bucks; they should be attempted only by lacemakers with considerable experience.

Fan 1

This has five ovals with a different floral motif in each. It has a ground of arcs rather than straight lines and it is a help to establish these lines at frequent intervals to keep the ground correct. Refer to Diag. 62a. Begin at *A* and establish *B C*. A thick gimp thread surrounds the ovals and it is sometimes necessary to carry threads with this to where they are needed; indeed this is usual practice. The honeycomb rings begin at *D* and work in both directions; sometimes the gimp will only surround one and at other times it will work several. As the rings are worked it is advisable to establish ground line *E F* as this will make the pattern easier to follow. You will notice that the ground is square at the bottom and diamond-shaped at the top. This does not affect the design in any way. Fig. 39 shows the oval complete.

Fan 2

This pattern is printed here in three parts (Diag. 63 a–c) and great care is needed when assembling them together to make a pricking. It resembles Chantilly and looks very attractive in black (half stitch). It has a central motif surrounded by scrolls with a honeycomb ground (Fig. 40; close-up view in Fig. 41); this centre piece makes an attractive dress inset on its own. There are many gimp threads needed and several extra pairs in the half stitch. Start at *A* and work in both directions as indicated to establish ground line *B C*. If the pattern is used as a dress inset, start at *E*.

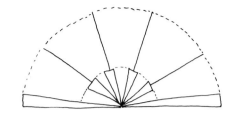

Diag. 61

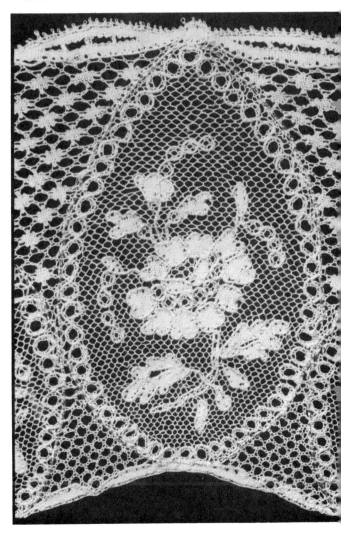

Fig. 39   *Detail from Fig. 37*

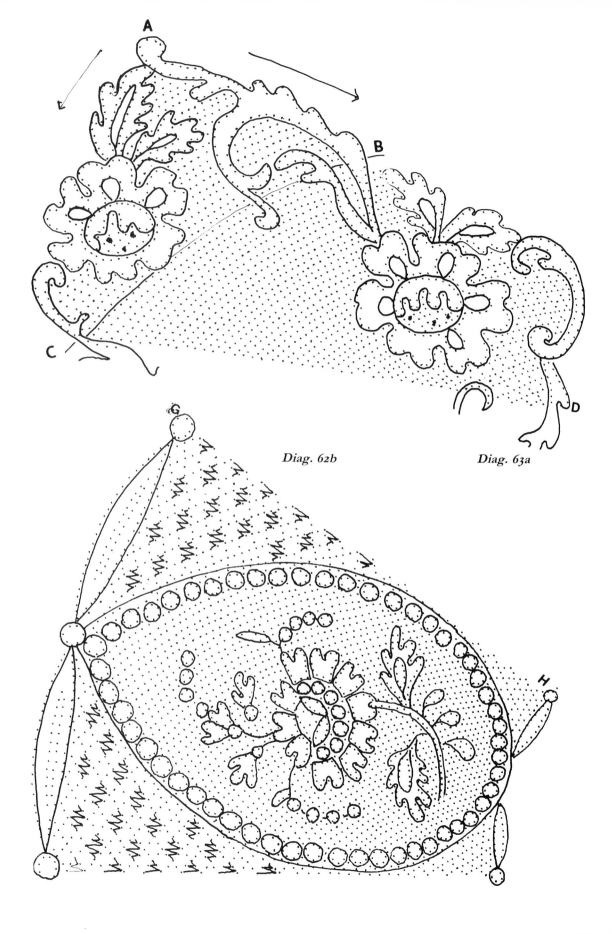

Diag. 62b   *Diag. 63a*

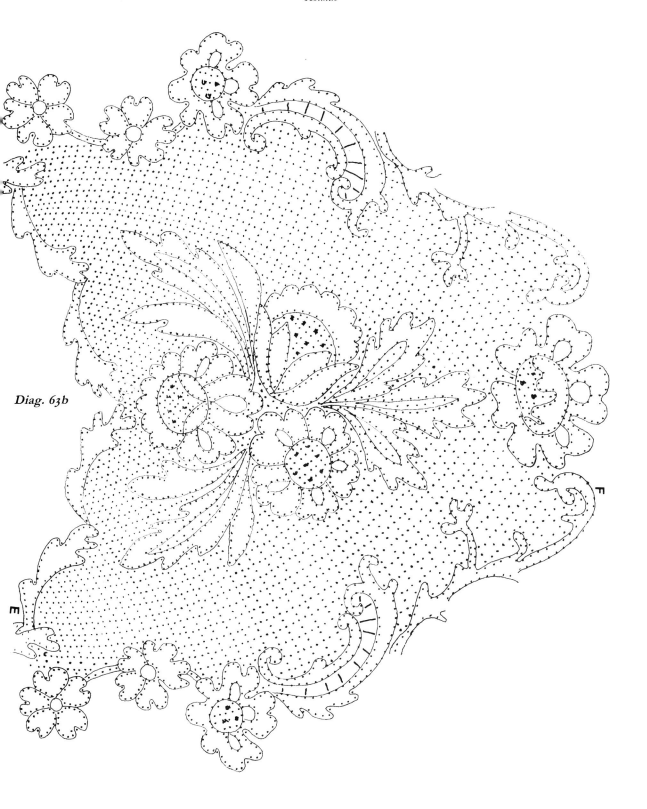

Diag. 63b

C

D

E

Diag. 63c

Fig. 40 (opposite, top) *Fan in black Bucks resembling Chantilly, half stitch, honeycomb and point ground; worked by Mrs Scotzen*

Fig. 41 (opposite, bottom) *Detail from Fig. 40*

Fig. 42 *Fan worked in Carrickmacross, cotton organdie applied to machine net and fillings embroidered on to the net*

Fig. 43 *Fan worked in needlepoint with bobbin lace backgrounds to the same design as Fig. 42*

Mounting the lace

Most antique lace fans were glued on to the sticks but the glue that was used sometimes damaged the lace. Use Evostik woodworking glue Resin W; and paint this on to the sticks, leaving it to dry about half an hour. Spread the sticks out in the position required and carefully place the lace on top. It will not stick immediately so there is plenty of time to fit it accurately. Pin down if necessary to an ironing board. Place a clean dry cloth over the lace and iron with a hot iron. Do not use steam. The lace will adhere to the surface of the sticks without sticking firmly. If the sticks have holes in them the lace can now be lightly sewn at the top. Be very careful as the sticks are brittle. The sticks can now be folded one by one and pressed. When the folding is complete, place elastic bands round the fan and leave it for a few days. When next you unfold it and fold it again the fan will fall naturally into place. Figs 42 and 43 shows two examples worked by the author.

FIVE

The uses of lace

Lace was used extensively in the nineteenth century on dress and household linen. Most articles were made in threads which laundered well; collars, cuffs and undersleeves were all detachable for this reason. Much of the creative design was found in accessories: fans, parasols, shawls and lappets were often made in silk. Lace is again fashionable today. More and more lacemakers produce their own pieces, and they want to show them off to their best advantage. This chapter contains ideas and patterns for the use of lace in different ways.

Dress

Edges, insets, yokes and motifs can all be used on dress as well as the usual collars (see Diag. 64).

1. Insets and edges of traditional design can be used on bodices and sleeves of dresses and blouses.
2. Motifs such as flowers or butterflies can be used as insets to form a neckline.
3. Yokes or bib collars can be made in contrast thread or in the threads taken from the material.
4. Ovals, diamonds or other shaped pieces can be inserted into neck lines.
5. Shaped pieces can be used as tie ends or jabots.
6. Triangular shaped godets can be inserted in a skirt.
7. Motifs can be used on a wrapover skirt: bold Bruges flowers for instance.
8. Motifs, circles or edges can be applied to pockets or used as bold designs on bags.
9. Daisy motifs can be used as a necklet or scattered on a yoke.
10. A narrow strip in colour can match a tie, applied below the knot.

Instead of using contrast threads it is possible to use threads that have been taken from the material to be made into the dress. Use natural fibres such as cotton, linen, silk or wool and wash the material first (if it is going to be a washable garment). Take the weft threads as these are the strongest and test their strengths by hand before considering this method.

It is also possible to use the warp threads of material while they are still attached either by taking out enough weft threads or using material straight from the loom with warp threads left at the end of weaving. These threads are wound on to bobbins and a lace pattern made either diagonally or in blocks as in Diag. 65. The threads will be left at the bottom but can be darned in or left as fringes or tassels. Work of this kind is most useful as the edge of a woven wall hanging, dress or jacket, lampshade, cushion, bag, place mats or tablecloth – there are many possibilities. There may be too many threads from the weaving to make an open pattern, and the surplus can be darned back before commencing. It is useful to pin the material edge to graph paper and then one can see the unwanted threads and plan the work.

Lace and knitting

Lace techniques can work very successfully within knitted or crocheted garments. The graphed design needs to be adapted to the wool size and Torchon is the best type to use. Larger bobbins are needed but I have used four- or six-inch nails: they work very well because of their weight. Wool needs a large amount of weight on the bobbin to get the tension right and it needs constant pulling while working.

The lace can be used in the same place as suggested for 'Dress' (above; see Diag. 66) but also in the following ways:

1. Circular edges can decorate the bottom of sleeves.
2. A circular edge can be used as a frilled collar (Diag. 83 can be used for this).

3. Lace can form an inset just behind the ribbing on a cardigan.

4. Edges can be made for knitted or crocheted shawls.

5. A square or triangle of Torchon can be greatly enlarged to make an entire shawl.

6. A shawl or stole can be made in wide Torchon strips (Diag. 66).

7. Baby dresses or jackets can be made entirely in lace – work out the lace pattern on graph paper to the pattern pieces.

Diag. 64

72

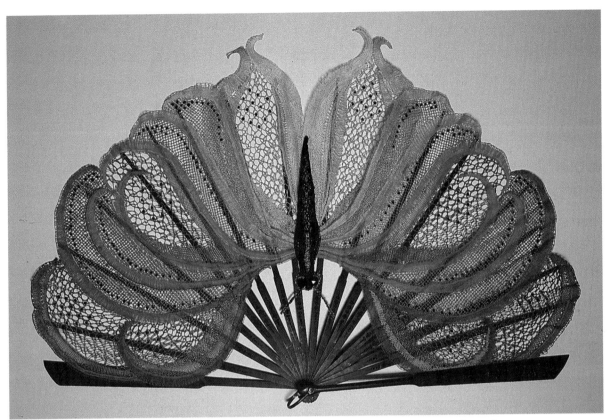

i *Butterfly fan worked in fine filament silks, stranded cotton, tinsel threads and jet beads*

ii Summer, *blue butterflies surrounded with daisies worked in Maltese leaves. The centres are a mass of french knots embroidered on simple cloth stitch middles*

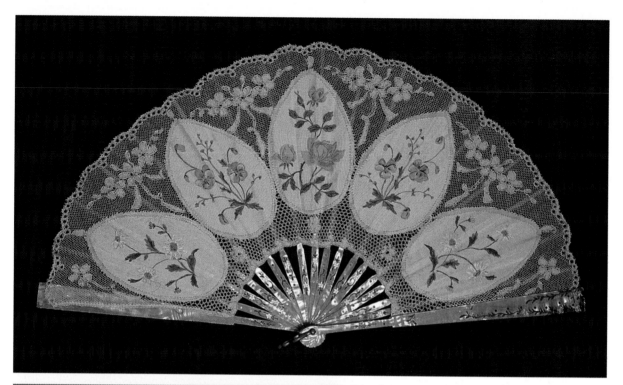

iii *Flower paintings on silk with Bucks lace worked in cream silk designed as a surround*

iv Tulips *by Eeva Lisa Kortalahti. Notice how the coloured threads are carried into the ground at the base*

v Adam and Eve *by Bridget Cook*

vi The Girl and the Peacocks
worked in silks

vii The Girl and the Horse *worked in coloured silks: the idea came from a visit to the Camargue*

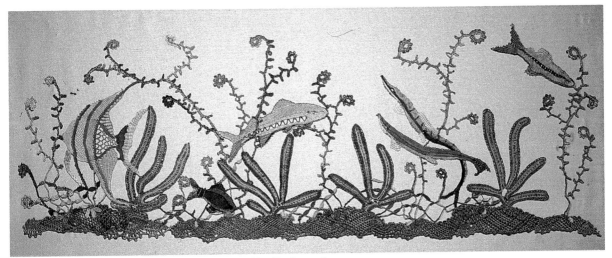

viii The Aquarium *worked in old Pearsall silk threads*

ix *Passion flower worked in three dimensions with a ladybird and a bee mounted on a tie-dyed background*

x *A wedding bouquet of three-dimensional flowers by Jean Spindlow*

xi *Three-dimensional orchid and fern leaf*

xii *Coloured Bedfordshire circle, worked by Margaret Lewis for a bag*

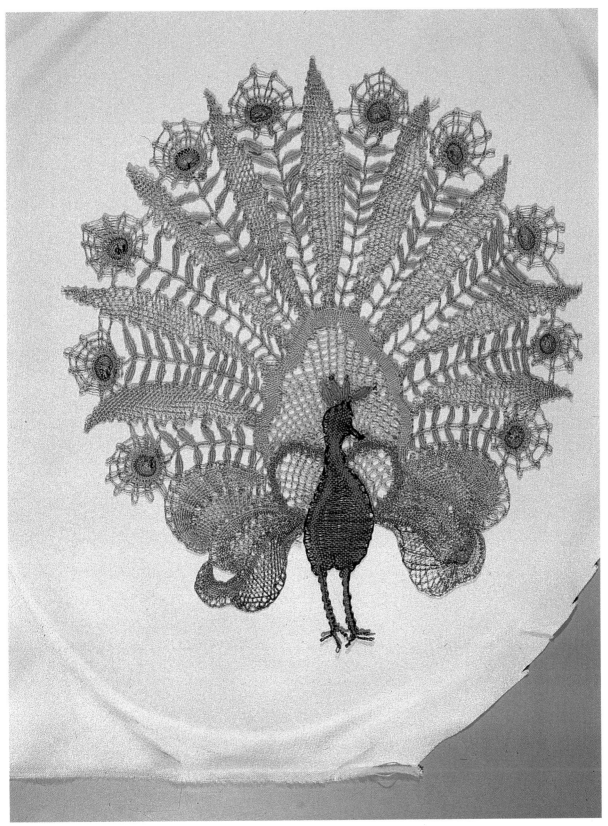

xiii *Stylized peacock worked in coloured Indian rayon threads*

xiv The Floral Dance; *pink and brown weavers give the colouring to the cream silk passives*

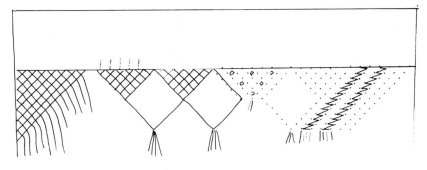

Diag. 65

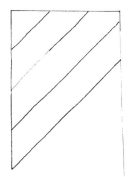

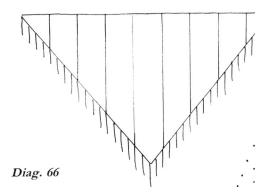

Diag. 66

Oval (24 pairs)

This oval has numerous uses and is very easy and quick to make (Diag. 67; Fig. 44). It is in Torchon with a thick gimp thread, Fil à Dentelle and Sylko Perle 5, but it can be worked in the threads of a material. It begins at *A* in Diag. 67 with four pairs and the rest are added as the oval increases and are taken out as they accumulate when the oval reduces.

Diag. 67

Uses

1. Three or five make insets in a neckline.
2. Seven or eight make a flower or a petalled lampshade (wired).
3. Four or six make a Christmas decoration (ball) (wired).
4. One makes a hair decoration attached to a clip or slide (wired).
5. Linked sideways, they make a bridal crown or a belt.
6. Reduced in size one oval will make an earring (wire surround).

Diagram 46 can be also used to make insets (24 pairs).

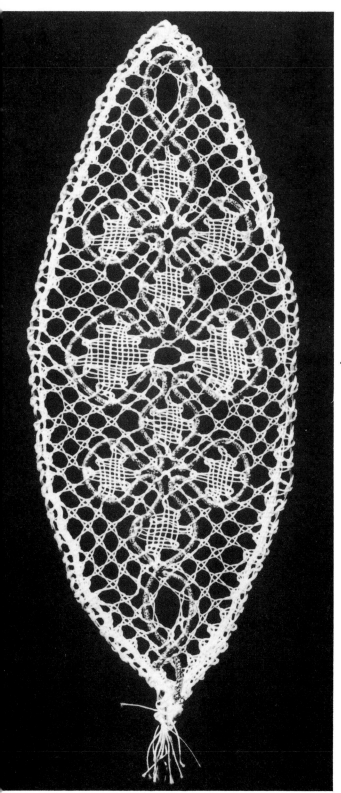

Diamond (*18 pairs*)

A simple butterfly inset is used as shown in Diag. 68. Heavy gimp is used to outline and the same threads as for the oval. Begin at *A* with four pairs and increase. Decrease to *B*. When the decorations are finished, tack them in position on the dress and pin stitch; or if the dress is to be washed often, attach with a wide machine zigzag. Most lace will wash very well and if firmly attached will even stand up to a washing machine. The material behind the lace can be either left in position or cut away.

Diag. 68

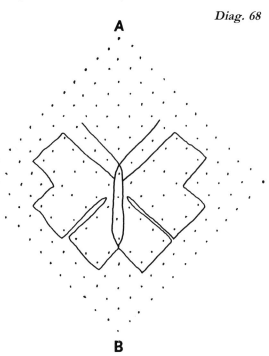

Dress yoke or bib collar (*120 pairs*)

Join the two pieces of pattern and begin at *A* in Diag. 69, work a narrow braid from *A* to *B* and add pairs where indicated. The blocks are in cloth and half stitch and it will be necessary to add pairs on the edge *BDE* and remove them as they accumulate on the inner edge *ACF*. This is unusual in Torchon patterns but the actual design and shape (Fig. 45) dictates this way of working and it is not difficult to do. Turn the pillow at *F* to *G* and work the other side. It will still be necessary to add and subtract pairs until the end.

Fig. 44 *Torchon oval to be used as a Christmas decoration ball*

Diag. 69

75

Fig. 45 *Bib yoke worked in the threads from the dress fabric so that there is an exact match, worked by Margaret Lewis*

Lace and patchwork

Squares of lace (Diag. 70) can be used as part of patchwork to form the inner square of (1) log cabin, or (2) cathedral window designs. Squares of ground stitches are all that is needed to give texture and pattern backed by material (Fig. 46). They can be worked in ribbon or other thick threads on a large scale for a cushion or bedspread.

Earrings

Small pieces of lace can be worked in Torchon or Bucks with a very fine thread to make a very decorative accessory (Diag. 71). Silver wire is used as an outer gimp thread and then attached to an earring wire or clip.

1. A simple half stitch strip is lightly twisted when finished to make a spiral.
2. A simple Torchon motif can be outlined with a heavy gimp.
3. A butterfly in Bucks with honeycomb wings can be outlined in silver gimp.

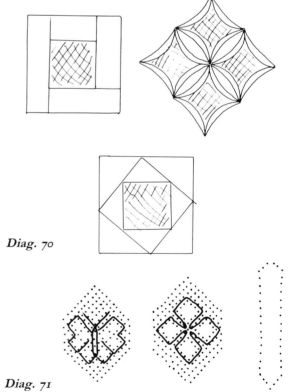

Diag. 70

Diag. 71

76

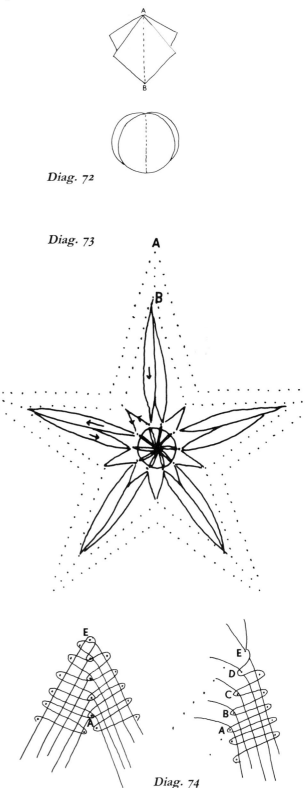

Diag. 72

Diag. 73

Diag. 74

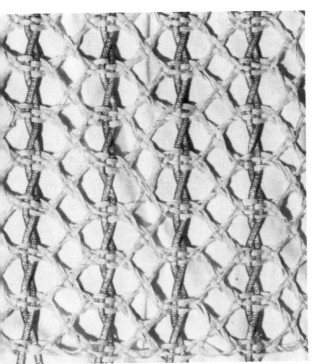

Fig. 46 *Ground worked in ribbon for a patchwork bed-spread*

Christmas decorations

Diag. 67 can be made into a solid or open ball for the tree and many of the small motifs can be used in this way if wired. Try making two or three diamonds from Diag. 68 and fold each one *A* to *B* joining them to each other as shown in Diag. 72. Circles will work in the same way using the circular motifs often made in Bucks. The poinsettia star can be used on its own or with two.

Poinsettia star

Work the star shape (Diag. 73) in gold thread with six pairs; start at holes *A* to *B*, work a braid back to *AB* and sew out. Make the sharp corners of the star (Diag. 74) by dropping pairs out from *A* to *D*, turning at *E* and picking them up again on the return rows *E* to *A* using the pin holes again. Make a circle of gold in the centre as in Diag. 3, Chapter One, and tie off. Sew in two pairs of red at *B* and make a long thin leaf to the centre; sew in and plait out to the star, sew in and make a leaf to the point, sew in and make a leaf to the centre and so on to the end; sew out.

This pattern when reduced in size makes a pretty earring.

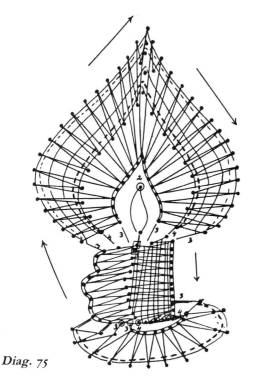

Diag. 75

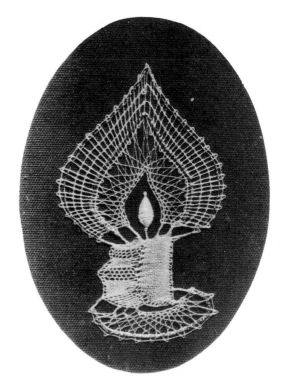

Fig. 47 Candle for Christmas *by Eeva Lisa Kortalahti*

Candle from Finland (12 pairs 50 Retour d'alsace and two gimps, thick and thin)

This design, by Eeva Lisa Kortalahti, makes a pretty Christmas card or, if suspended in a wire ring, a tree decoration or window mobile. Diag. 75 and Fig. 47 are self-explanatory.

Lampshades

Lampshades are excellent in lace, which can be used not only for trimmings but for complete shades or panels. Any form of lace can be used and the play of light through the lace adds to its transparency and shows it off to advantage. It is also just as pleasing unlit. It need not be 'pretty' and suitable just for a bedroom, but in coarse colourful textured threads can fit in any room. Designs can be abstract, pictorial, geometric or floral, but as with fans one needs the frame first. There are many different shapes on the market and with some imagination, real individuality can be given to a lampshade using traditional patterns. It can be designed to match the lamp base or the furnishings of the room. Many people are cautious of making a shade because of the technique of lining it – the inner lining of a lampshade in lace is very import-

ant. Lace unlined gives too much light and the bulb is visible. The lace can form the outer layer of a shade or be attached to material; this depends on the type of lace and on personal preference. Many plain lampshades can be bought ready-made, and one's own lace attached, but it is very satisfying to make the lot and in doing so one can get a better match.

To make lining

Bind the struts of the frame with tape; the top and bottom are the most important ones. Work out the shape of the pattern pieces by pinning old sheeting to the top and bottom of the frame (Diag. 76) with the straight of grain as shown. Pin opposite corners first and then the rest, keeping it very tight with no wrinkles. Pin also to the down struts and when satisfied mark the seam lines with a pen. You may need two, three, four or five panel seams or, in the case of a drum or cone, only one. Remove the sheeting and use this as the pattern for the lining and the lace. Cut it out in the chosen material with the correct grain and seam by machine or back stitch. Fit it onto the frame again making the seams fit to the down struts and again pin firmly to the frame as shown. Stitch firmly with a close oversew from right to left with a double matching thread to the top and bottom. Trim away the excess material back to the stitches. Make another lining in the same way and attach to the inside. Bring the inner edges over the outer stitches and oversew in the same way. Trim again. These seams are covered with braid, binding or with the edge of the lace.

Drum shapes

These can be easily made by using a ring for top and bottom and the shape cut in a proprietary iron-on lamp parchment that can be covered in material.

A rectangle is used for a drum, and a half-circle for a cone.

Suggestions for lace on lamps

1. As petals on an Art Nouveau shade.
2. Alternate panels (pictorial scenes, geometric or floral designs).
3. Applied to material before making up (Islam pattern).
4. Extensions of woven material.
5. A separate ring of lace that slots into the base of a hanging lamp. Attach it to another lamp ring so that the bulb can be changed if necessary.
6. Torchon insets alternating with material.
7. Cones made from half circle fan patterns.
8. 'Tiffany' lamp.

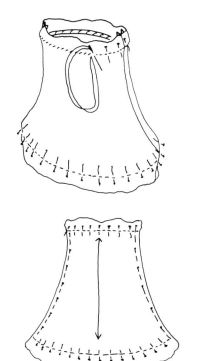

Diag. 76

Diag. 77

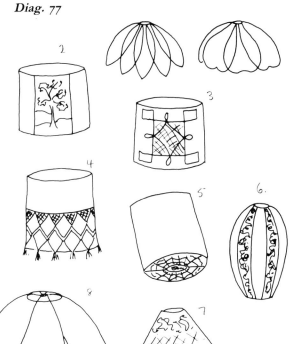

The following patterns fit together to make a parasol (8 ovals), a 'Tiffany' lamp (7 ovals) or a round cloth or mat with a star-shaped centre (12 ovals). The girl oval is easier than the flower oval.

Flower oval (Bucks)

This (Diag. 78) has the same flower design as in the earlier fan (Diag. 62a), but the oval is of a different shape. To make the full pattern (Fig. 48) it is joined by the triangles 1 or 2 at *C* to *B*.

Begin at *A* with four pairs and increase to ten pairs where the two braids divide. The design has honeycomb rings inside a cloth braid and pairs added as required from *A* to *C* (62 pairs). It will be necessary to add extra pairs in the flower buds, leaves and petals to keep a solid form, removing them later. Decrease pairs in the braids as they accumulate from *C* to *B*. Finish with the minimum number of pairs at *B* and tie off. Make another oval and then sew in pairs from *C* to *B* on one side; work the triangle, and sew the pairs out on the other side; tie off.

Triangle 1

Sew in pairs as they are required and work honeycomb ground with mayflowers where indicated (Diag. 79). The outer edge is in cloth stitch with a twist to the centre. The finished article can have a narrow shell edge attached to this if desired.

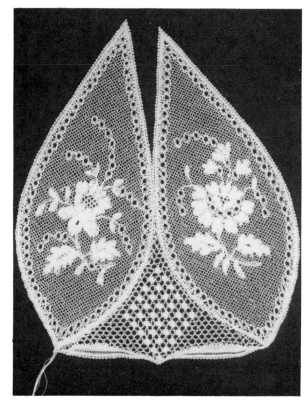

Fig. 48   *Two ovals joined with a triangular piece to make a parasol or Tiffany lampshade*

Diag. 78

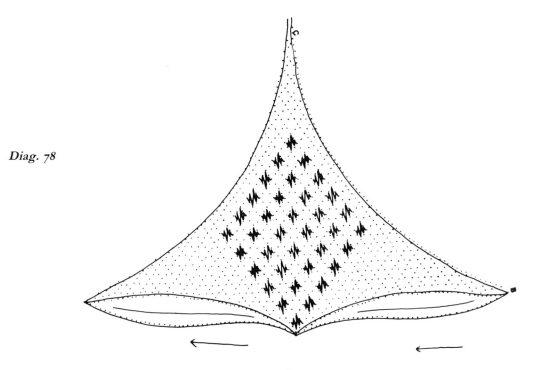

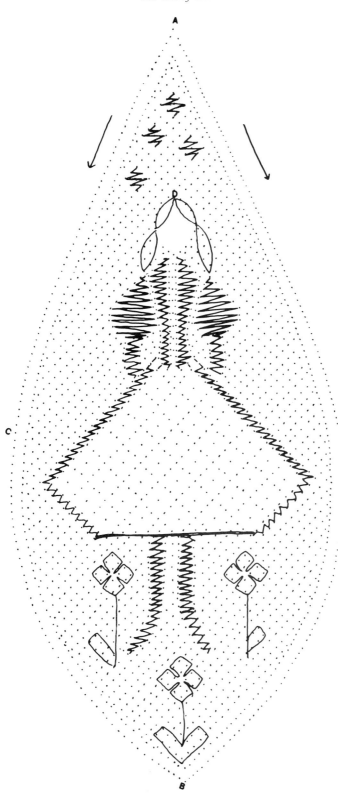

Diag. 79

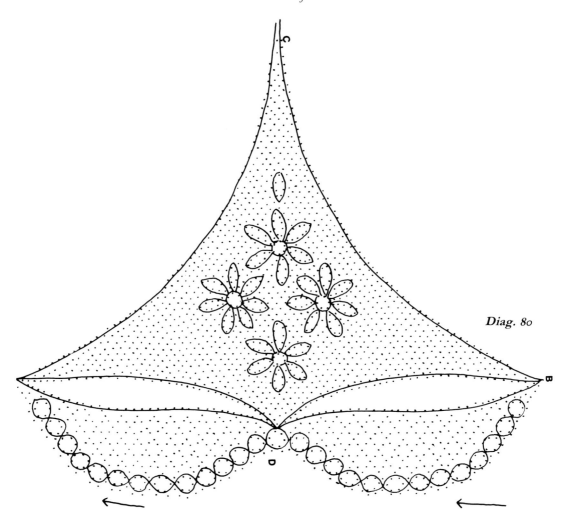

Diag. 80

Triangle 2

This has a point ground with cloth stitch daisies with honeycomb centres (Diag. 80). The large leaves can be cloth stitch or half stitch and the outer scallop has honeycomb with rings on the outer edge. Allow the pairs to accumulate in the deep indent *D* and do not remove – they are needed for the next scallop. When working this triangle with the ovals, it is easier to make all the ovals first and then all the triangular fillings; the threads from the scallop can then be followed through.

Girl oval

Begin at *A* (Diag. 81) in the same way as for the flower oval but with no ring. Add four pairs at *D* and make leaves to the shoulders; leave hanging. Work the face in cloth stitch over these. Begin the sleeves with the pairs from the leaves. The sleeves are in half stitch; the jacket is in cloth and twist, and any stitch can be used for the skirt, a different one for each. The flowers are in cloth surrounded by a gimp and there are a few half stitch mayflowers to shade the top above the head. This pattern is more like Torchon and has no gimp surround. Fig. 49 shows the completed oval.

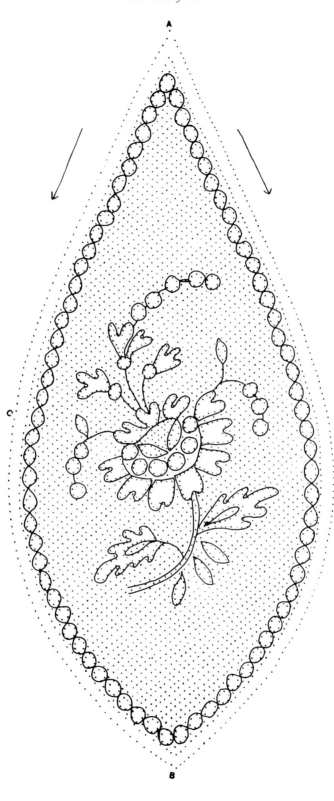

Diag. 81

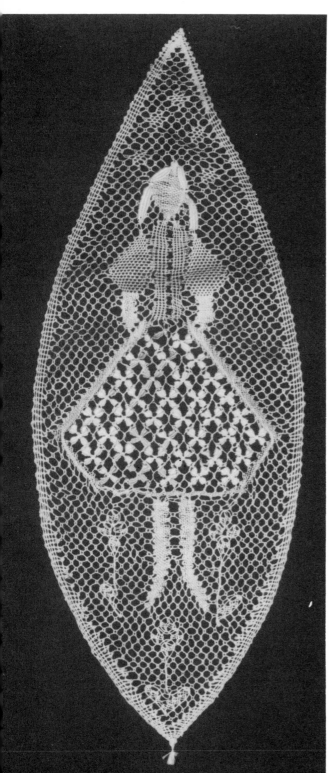

Useful edges 1

This is a very quick scallop edge (Diag. 82) for use on parasols or lamps and has been used on the zodiac parasol, the dress yoke and the floral dance. It can be worked with alternating colours very successfully.

Diag. 82

Useful edges 2

This water lily oval edge from Finland (27 pairs 100 linen; Diag. 83) makes a very attractive edge to an oval mat. It can be enlarged to make an oval cloth or it can be adapted to form a frilled collar or edge to knitted garments. See Fig. 50.

The working is easily done from the diagram. Both patterns joined make a quarter-oval.

Fig. 49 *Oval with a Torchon figure to be used in a similar way as in Fig. 48*

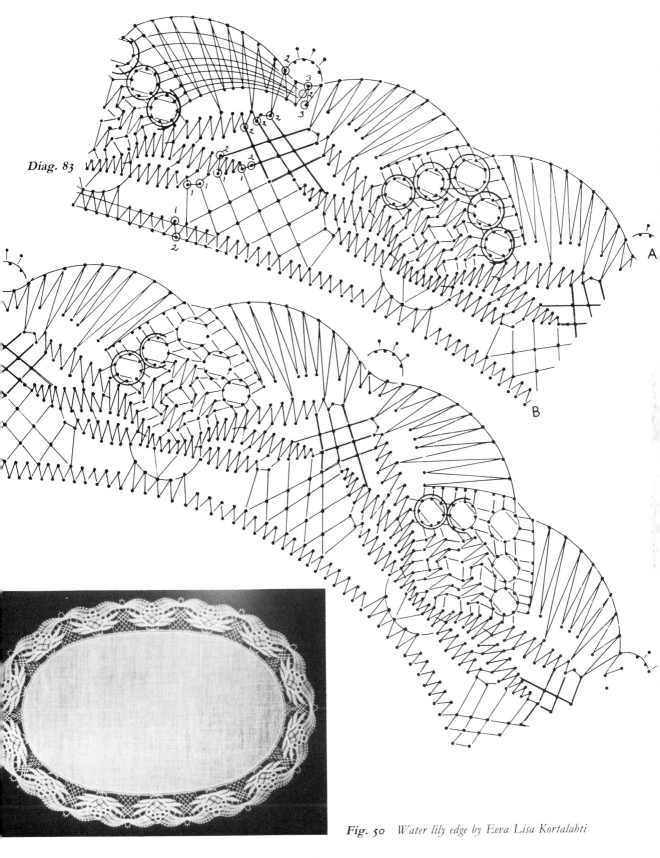

Diag. 83

Fig. 50 *Water lily edge by Eeva Lisa Kortalahti*

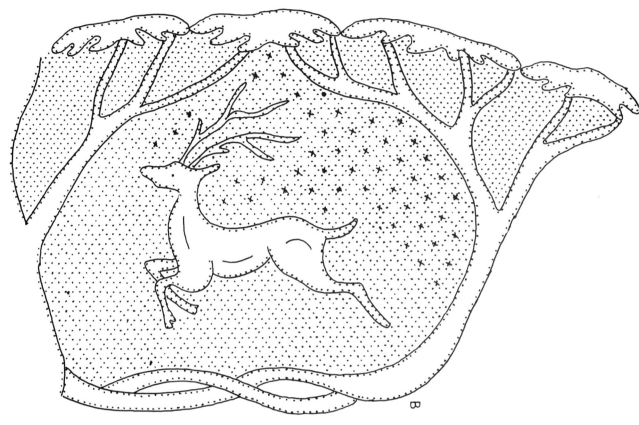

Diag. 84   **Fig. 51** (opposite)   *Deer mat: a year in the life of a deer*

Patterns by request

I have been requested on many occasions to include the deer pattern and the zodiac from my earlier *Creative Design in Bobbin Lace*, and they have been adapted to fit the pages of the present book.

The deer

This has been planned (Diag. 84) as a repeat motif; eight will make the round. The original had eight different deer but this has only the one – Fig. 51 shows the worked pattern. Different ones can however be put in for variety by drawing them in yourself.

Match the repeat diagram to form the round and start on the tree *A* to *B*. It is worked as Bucks floral and care must be taken with the direction of work in the cloth areas. Mayflowers have been used as shading and the antlers are double gimps. Twists can be used in the body as indicated.

The Zodiac

This was originally designed as a parasol but I have put the zodiacal signs into rounds (Fig. 52) so that they can be used for pictures, box tops, cloth insets, mobiles, etc. The pattern can be enlarged to fit whatever is required and the thread chosen to fit the pricking. The ones shown can be in DMC *retour d'alsace* 50. They all have honeycomb ground, a gimp surround and an outer cloth and twist edge. Where there is only a single row of dots but two pieces of cloth joining, the weavers from both sides meet. This happens only where two pieces lie adjacent as in the centre of the goat's head, the sleeve of virgo and the huntsman's body and quiver. The signs can, if you wish, be redrawn into the ovals of Diag. 81 and made into a cloth or mat.

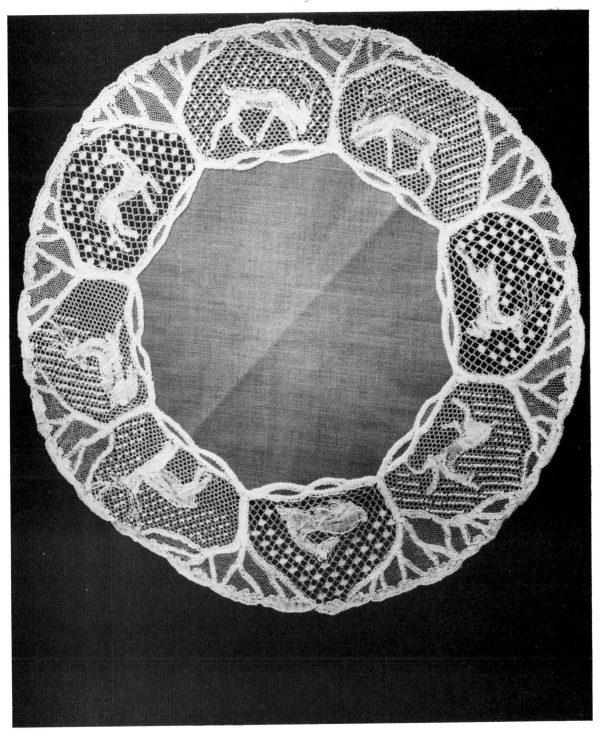

Fig. 52 *Zodiac parasol*

Diag. 85

Diag. 87

Capricorn

Cloth and twist for the tail, cloth stitch for horns and body surround. Part of the face in half stitch and his beard in cloth and twist. The inner body is Maltese leaves. See Diag. 85.

Sagittarius

Face and body in cloth stitch, hair and horse tail in cloth and twist; quiver in half stitch and bow in double gimp. See Diag. 86.

Cancer

Cloth stitch claws alternating with half stitch, legs in alternating cloth and half stitch, shell body edge in cloth with a filling of bias ground. See Diag. 87.

Gemini

Cloth and twist for hair, cloth stitch for face, hands and feet, half stitch for sleeves and dress outer, cloth and twist for waistcoat and rose ground in the skirts. See Diag. 88.

Diag. 86

Diag. 88

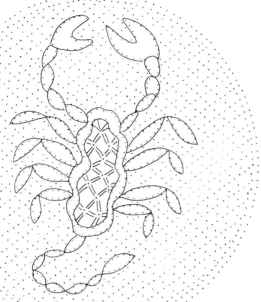

Diag. 91

Scorpio
Worked as for Cancer but with spider filling. See Diag. 89.

Libra
Cloth stitch with a half stitch base; the pans are half stitch inners and cloth stitch outers. See Diag. 90.

Taurus
All cloth stitch with half stitch ears. See Diag. 91.

Aries
Cloth stitch is used for face and legs with cloth and twist horns. The body has numerous tallies to make a thick woolly coat. The horn will need three gimps. See Diag. 92.

Diag. 90

Diag. 92

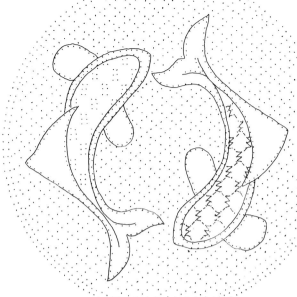

Diag. 93

Diag. 95

Virgo

Work the leaves first to a plaited stalk. Move down from *A* to *B* and back *B* to *C*. Tie off the leaves and leave the cut-off threads to take through the ground afterwards for tying off. Push the pins flat and work the round over the top. The hair is in cloth and twist, the face, hands and feet in cloth, the sleeves in half stitch, and the dress in cloth, cloth and twist and half stitch over the top of the Maltese leaves. See Diag. 93.

Leo

The mane is in cloth stitch with the front legs in half stitch and the back surround in cloth with a may-flower inner. See Diag. 94.

Pisces

Cloth and twist is used for the tail and fins with whole stitch block filling. See Diag. 95.

Aquarius

Cloth and twist for hair, cloth stitch for face, arms and legs; the pot is half stitch with some areas of half stitch with gimps as shown to indicate water. The dress is in cucumber (cloth trails with tallies). See Diag. 96.

Diag. 96

Diag. 94

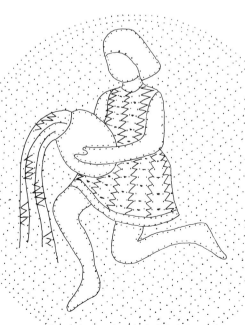

SIX

Modern interpretations

When lace techniques are used to interpret a drawing, there are no fixed rules. One needs to use all the lacemaking techniques available to create the desired effect. If it will not work by one method then try another; it is quite feasible even to invent a method, for after all, lace-making has progressed and evolved only by the ingenuity of workers through the centuries.

Figures and animals

These are difficult to work in lace because they are flat interpretations of something which is solid and three dimensional, and one has to think as an artist to give the picture depth. Where he would use colour we have to use stitches. Many techniques are involved in the making of realistic eyes, hair, hands and clothing, and this is even more difficult in a one-piece lace. They can be interpreted in a simple way as in Fig. 49 or Fig. 53 where stitches are used as the dress patterning but the figures appear flat. The Czech interpretations, Figs. 54–58, show the use of stitches to give an illusion of figure shape; Figs. 59 and 60 are figures in thread and become art forms with plenty of movement and character depicted. The Figures from Finland (Figs. 61 and 62) are different again in their interpretation and show the need for artistic drawing.

More detailed figures can be worked in mixed lace techniques with sewings and large areas divided into workable parts. Dresses have large areas which need dividing into panels of cloth and half stitch to give shading and they can have three-dimensional details such as frills, scales and ribbons worked first and the rest worked over the top.

Fig. 53 *Girl on a swing worked in mixed lace by Valerie Hook*

Fig. 54 (opposite, left) Woman at Work *by B. Hanusova*

Fig. 55 (opposite, right) Woman at Work *by B. Hanusova*

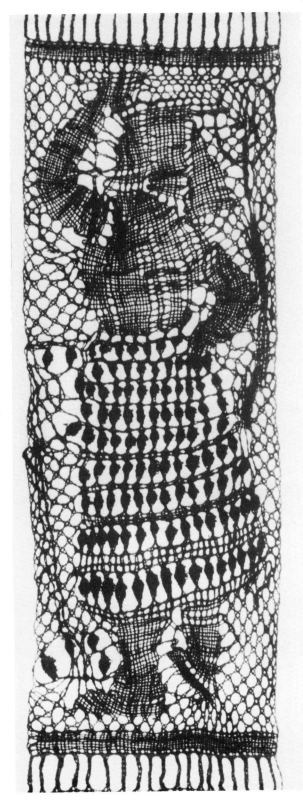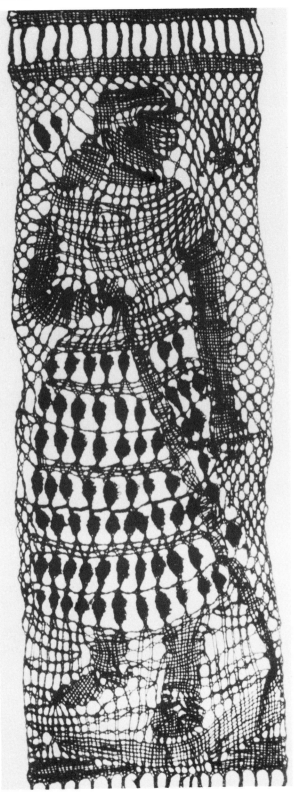

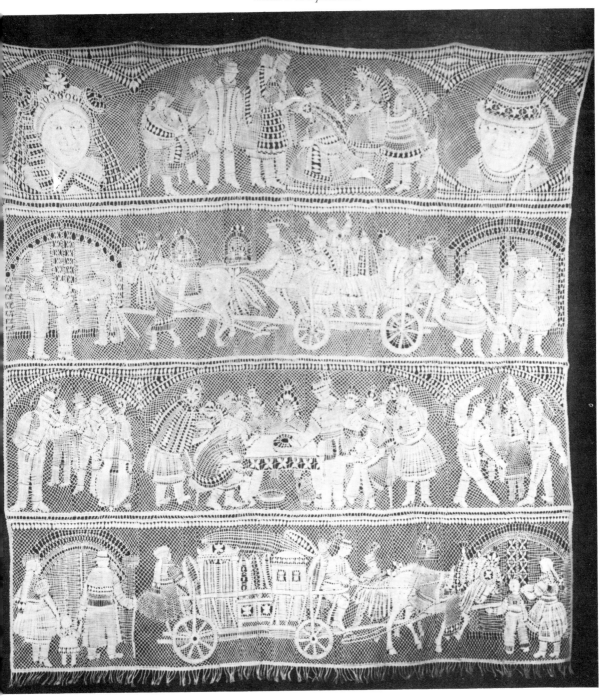

Fig. 56   Easter *by B. Hanusova*

Fig. 57   The Village Wedding *by B. Hanusova (the property of the Museum of Lace, Vamberk)*

95

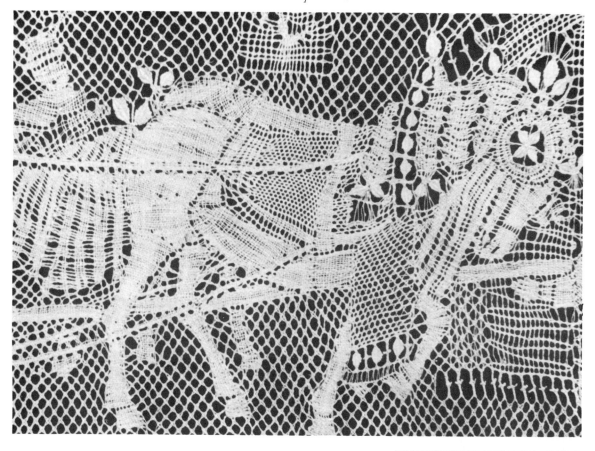

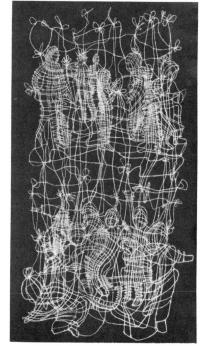

Fig. 58   *Detail from Fig. 57*

Fig. 59   Voices of Happy Children *by Marie Vankova Kuchynkova (70cm × 40cm) worked in natural and red linen by Jana Stefkova*

Fig. 60 (opposite)   *Detail from Fig. 59*

Fig. 61 Madonna *by Eeva Lisa Kortalahti*   **Fig. 62** Guardian Angel *by Eeva Lisa Kortalahti*

Faces

These are best worked in cloth stitch detailed by the use of twists, holes, four-pin buds or spiders to make the features. Side faces are easier than frontals because, being worked from top to bottom, the curve of the cheek and chin are formed as the threads are brought round for the neck and the eye is the only feature required. Work with a twisted edge and no foot as this gives a softer appearance; it is often better to leave the face blank, with no features, and when finished move the threads with a pin to give an illusion of a face as in the dancing girl, Fig. 31.

Fig. 63 *Face detail from Fig. 57*

Fig. 64 (opposite) *Head, a study for* The Village Wedding *(Fig. 57) but not used by B. Hanusova*

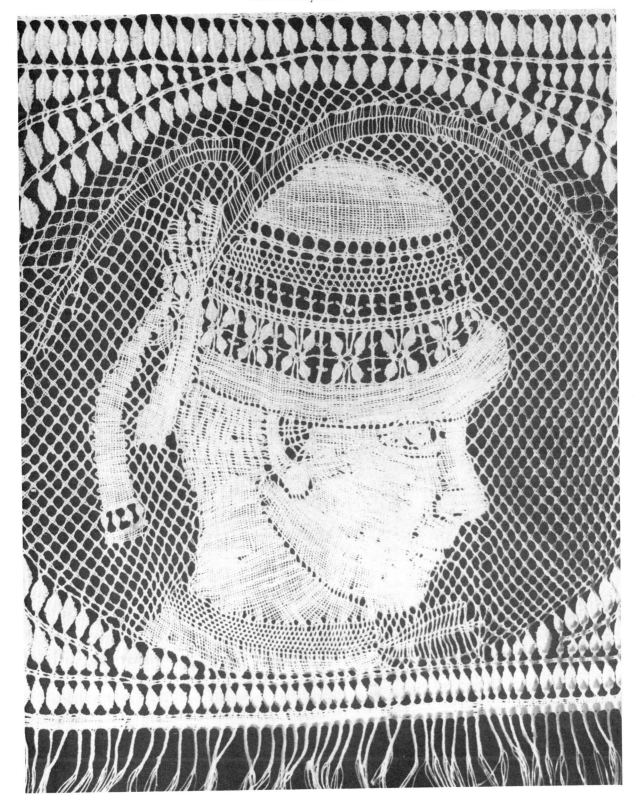

Hands

These are worked in cloth stitch with twists between groups of passives to form the finger separation. If possible it is best to work from the fingers to the wrist to prevent the loss of outline at the finger tip.

Diag. 97

Fig. 65 *Head detail from the Girl and the Peacocks*   **Fig. 66** *Head and hand detail from the Girl and the Horse*

Hair

This can be worked in cloth stitch and twisted cloth to give the shaded effect that occurs in hair. It can be worked simply as in Fig. 53, with three-dimensional tendrils as in the Fig. 65, or flowing as in Fig. 67. Simple hair formations are shown with leaves depicting plaits or bunches, breaking out into cloth and twist as in Diag. 98, or in tendrils worked in the direction shown in Diag. 99, with the face line marked in dots to allow the hair to lie over the face on the right side.

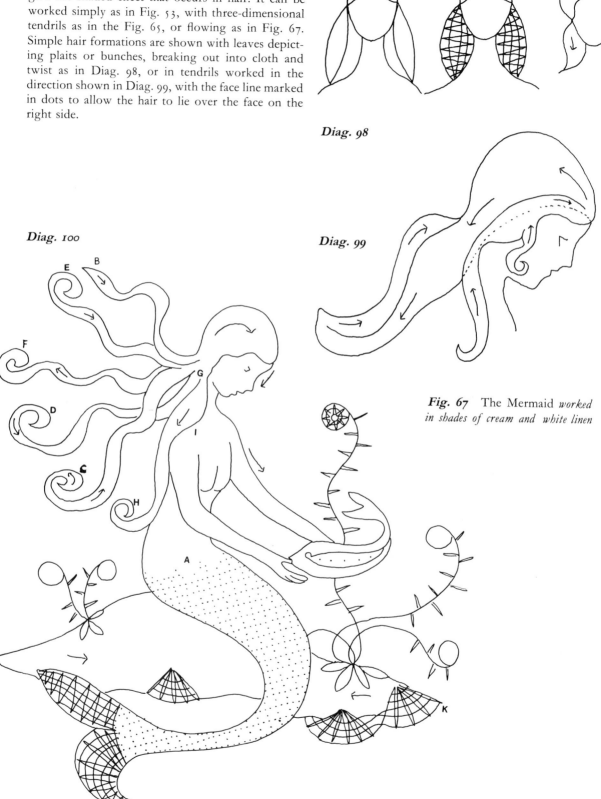

Diag. 98

Diag. 100

Diag. 99

Fig. 67   The Mermaid *worked in shades of cream and white linen*

The mermaid

Diag. 100 can be enlarged to make it workable in thicker threads, and it can be worked in a silky thread for the body and in textured threads for the rocks. The size of thread will depend on the enlargement (see Figs. 67 and 68).

Begin by working the honeycomb scales on the tail from *A* and leave some of these threads hanging for the tail fin. Start the hair at *B*, *C*, and *D* and bring the threads round the head to start the face. Other tendrils start at *E* and out to *F* sewing in where necessary. Some threads that are surplus at *G* work out to *H*. Work down the face with a hole for an eye and down to the neck and shoulders; any surplus threads from the hair can be left out and taken in at *I*. Divide for the

Fig. 68 *Detail from Fig. 67*

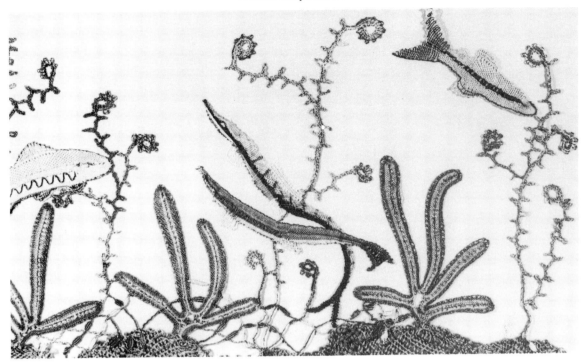

Fig. 69 *Detail from fish panel*

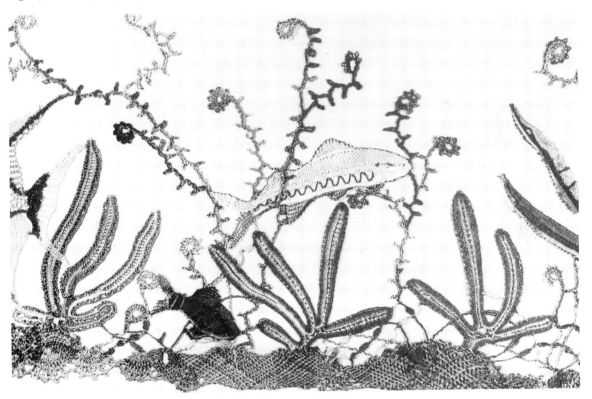

Fig. 70 *Detail from fish panel*

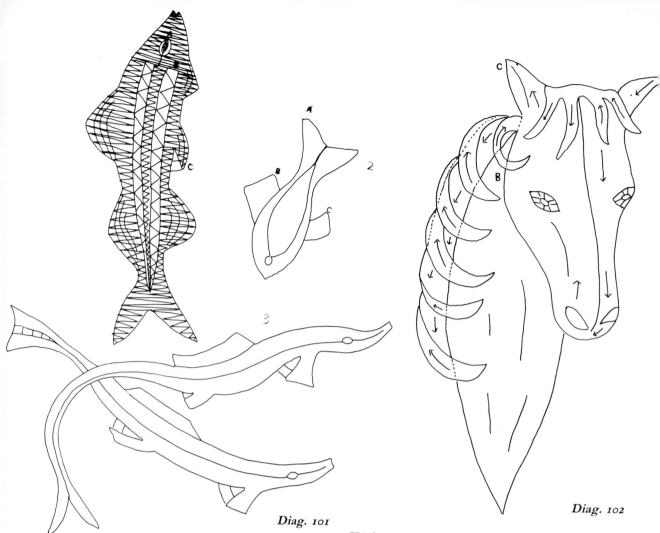

Diag. 101

Diag. 102

Fish

arms and bosom and work one arm down to sew into the fish later and one down to the fingers also to sew out into the fish. The threads from the upper body are carried over the arm with others sewn into the arm to change into half stitch for the tail. This is worked over the honeycomb sewing into it at the edges. All the threads are used for the tail fin in twisted cloth stitch. The fish is a tape which begins at the tail with twists and curves round the head to sew out near the tail; the filling is spiders worked with these threads. The reeds are made by a series of plaits which go out from side to side and back to the main plait with sewings; they end in a cloth and twist ring to form a flower. The flower in the mermaid's hair is a round from Chapter One (see p. 10) applied afterwards.

The rock is worked from *J* and *K* to the body where it is sewn out. The threads from the rock break into Torchon shells at intervals for scallops and the reeds are attached by leaves on the rock.

The fish panel (Figs 69 and 70) was worked in a similar way but in colour with a variety of tropical fish (many books will provide inspiration).

1. Start at the mouth; two pairs are added at *A* for the eye and divide into three trails at B, nine pairs in the lower trail, four pairs in the centre and seven pairs in the upper trail. Change to cloth and twist for the fins and tail and leave the pairs from fin *C* to be taken back into the body.

2. Start at *A* (in Diag. 101) in cloth and twist and work to the fin B. Add four pairs at B, work cloth and twist to meet the other threads, join all together and work down to the head, turn and work the other side. Work the fin on the other side and leave four pairs out again at *C* and tie off. Finish at the tail end with minimal pairs and work a filling in the centre.

3. These start at the tail and turn at the mouth; by changing the weaver colour on alternate rows, stripes can be achieved.

The horse's head

This has a three-dimensional mane which is worked first. The fronds work up as shown and return in half stitch. The head is then worked in two halves with sewings, starting at *A*, turning at the nose with holes for the nostrils. The eyes are spiders and as pairs accumulate above the eye, they can be left out for the neck at *B*. The ear at *C* is half in cloth stitch and half in half stitch to form the shading. Add more pairs to the head with sewings to complete the neck which is worked over the fronds but attached with sewings to the half stitch.

Birds

1. This is worked from beak to tail, adding two pairs for the tally in the eye, keeping pin holes close under the neck and opening out on the top of the head so that the threads will swing round to be straight and level by the time the neck is reached. It may be necessary to use pins twice to do this. Work in cloth stitch with twists where marked and end at *B* in Diag. 103 with two leaves. Work narrow braids for the tail, stem stitch for the head fronds, and narrow braids for the feet and legs all sewn into the body. Make the wing in alternate half and cloth stitch from *C* to *D* and tie off; then work the other wing from *E* to the body.
2. This is the peacock with the tail down, in Fig. 42 and Diag. 103. Start at *A*, and with a hole for an eye, work down to *B*, turn and work *C* in half stitch or any other filling to sew out at *X*. Sew in pairs at *D*, work down to *E* and turn, work *F* in half stitch or any other filling to *G*, sew out. Sew in pairs at *H* and work to *I*, divide, and work one half down to *J* and tie off; work the other half down to *K*, turn and half stitch *L* to *X*, sew out. Work foot from *M* to *N* and foot from *O* to *P*.

The peacock

This has been worked in white and in colour with very little difference in the working (Fig. 73).

Begin with two pairs for each claw making six pairs for each leg and work up to the body meeting the weavers and adding two more pairs at *A* in Diag. 104. Work the body with occasional twists in the weaver as indicated. Decrease to ten pairs after the beak has been worked and make five leaves to finish at *B*. Pin flat and work the wings on either side of the body. Start at *C* with four pairs and increase to nine; twist the weavers in the centre each time to make a vein. Sew to the body and turn at *D*; reduce to seven pairs, work to *E*, turn and work *F* in half stitch. Sew out. Sew in seven

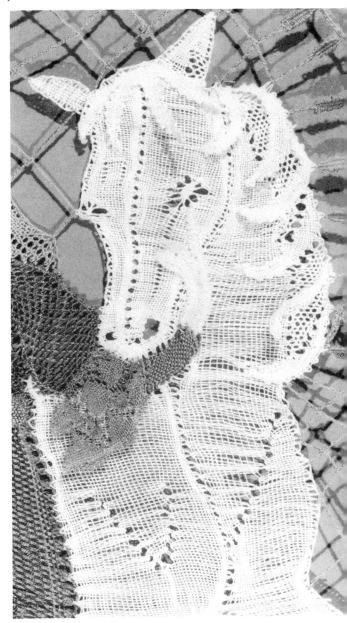

Fig. 71 *Horse's head: detail from the Girl and the Horse*

Diag. 103

pairs at *G*, work to *H*, turn and work *I* in half stitch, and sew out. These threads can be carried over for the trail at *K*. Sew in pairs from *G* to *J* for the Torchon ground of the lower tail and pairs for the leaves that form the upper tail, *K* to *L* (Diag. 105). Make a round as in Chapter One (page 10), forming its centre and its shape to create an ellipse. The number of twists will need adjusting to achieve this. Use two pairs from the sewn-off round to make a plait from the centre to *M*; make windmill crossings with the leaves as each is

reached. The trail from *K* accommodates the threads which go in and out for the Torchon lower tail and the plait and half stitch which go in and out for the upper tail – these are worked simultaneously. The Torchon ground sews into the body until the neck is reached. At this point the threads cross the head and work in and out of a small trail that lies across the head (Diag. 105); this leaves the head free on the right side. Continue round the tail adding extra pairs for extra leaves and taking them and the others in and out

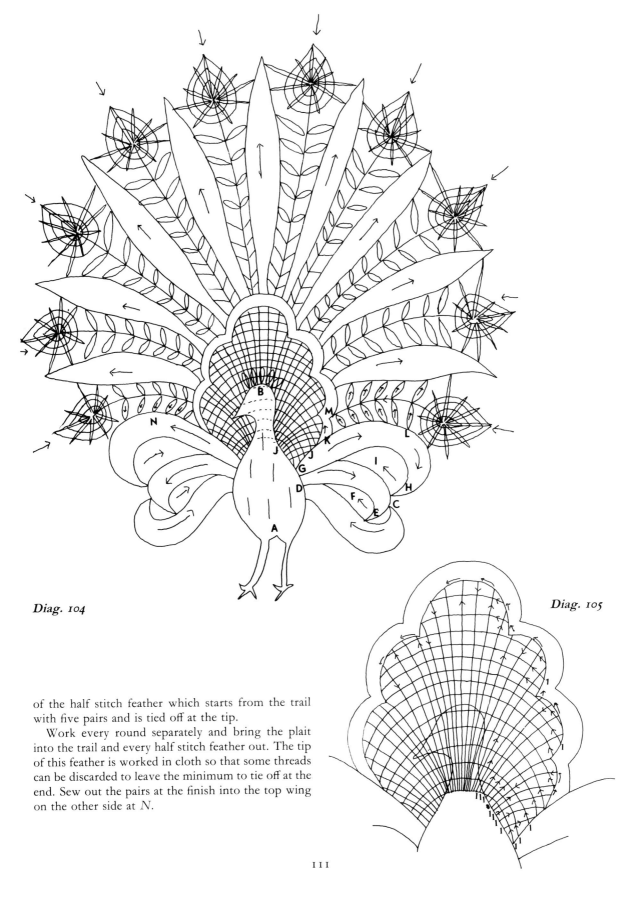

Diag. 104

Diag. 105

of the half stitch feather which starts from the trail with five pairs and is tied off at the tip.

Work every round separately and bring the plait into the trail and every half stitch feather out. The tip of this feather is worked in cloth so that some threads can be discarded to leave the minimum to tie off at the end. Sew out the pairs at the finish into the top wing on the other side at *N*.

Using colour

The colour of the weaver usually dominates the piece being worked and this can be used to great advantage as in the coloured butterfly. The peacock has a blue body, a gold/yellow lower tail and a combination of bright green and gold/brown upper tail. The leaves have been woven with the green but each leaf consists of one pair green and one pair gold/brown. This gives a greeny gold mixture for the half stitch feather. The eyes in the feathers were rounds using brown/gold for weaver and outer pair, with two pairs turquoise and two pairs mauve as inners.

Coloured butterfly

The principle of this butterfly is the same as for the bird in Fig. 71. Work down, turn and come back with a filling but as the weaver and the passives are changed gradually, a colour change takes place from yellow through to mauve. It could work from yellow through to blue mixing the colours as one would do on a palette.

The body

Begin with the antennae as in Diag. 106, work to the head and add more pairs. Work down to divide at *A* and make two braids; add two pairs as indicated for tallies. Work another body in reverse as in Chapter Two (page oo) and when finished pad lightly. Beads can be inserted instead of tallies.

Underwing

Begin at *A* in Diag. 107 with yellow weavers and yellow passives, work to *B*, turn, and change to half stitch. At *C* change to a gold weaver and at *D* discard the gold weaver and use a pink one. This gives a slight orange tone. Work from *F* to *G* with pink weavers and yellow passives; also from *H* to *I* and from *I* to *J*. The filling at *K* is in a fine yellow/pink combined.

Upper wing

Begin at *A* in Diag. 108 with pink and yellow combined, turn at *B*, work to *C*, and leave the threads hanging for the filling at *D*. Work *E* to *F* with pink passives and a red weaver and change to a pink weaver at *F* to work up to *G*. The filling at *H* is worked with pink threads and the filling at *D* can be finished off. *I* has red weavers and some red passives and a few mauve ones; the same threads work from *J* to *K*

Fig. 72 (opposite) *Detail of bird from the Girl and the Peacocks*

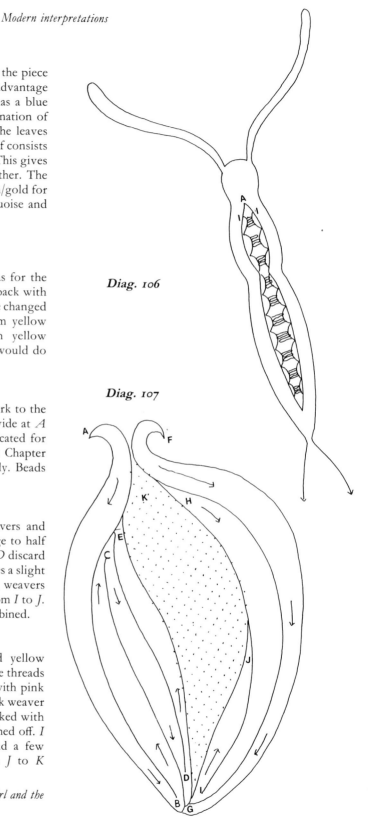

Diag. 106

Diag. 107

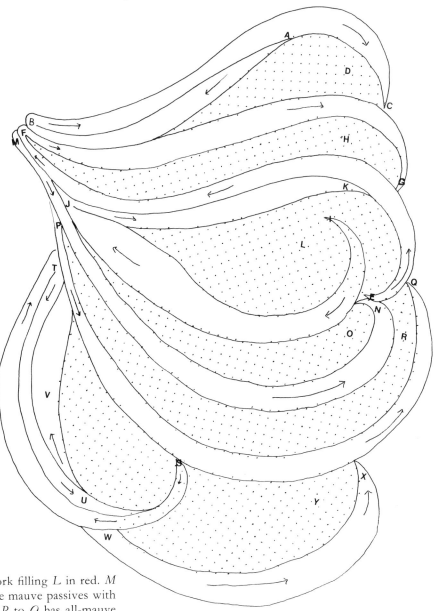

Diag. 108

sewing in where necessary. Work filling *L* in red. *M* to *N* has red weavers and more mauve passives with filling *O* in red/mauve mixed. *P* to *Q* has all-mauve passives and red weavers with the filling in pale mauve at *R*. *S* to *T* has mauve passives and red weaver, *T* to *U* mauve passives and mauve weaver and *V* in half stitch. *W* to *X* has mauve passives and a red weaver, with a darker mauve filling in *Y* which crosses the feather tip *S*. The filling stitches work from side to side wherever possible, and can be of any kind. Torchon is marked in this example.

This butterfly was designed to fit fan sticks, but it can be enlarged to whatever size required. The threads used were silk, fine enough to allow the doubling of threads for colour combinations and to give a sheen.

Fig. 73 *Stylized peacock*

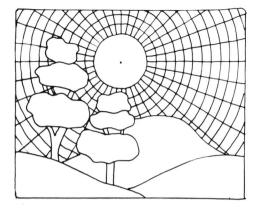

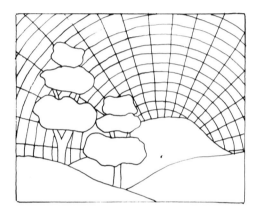

Buildings

Architectural structures are very interesting to work; they can be worked in a one-piece lace as in the Floral Dance (Fig. 35) or as in the work illustrated from Czechoslovakia, with their structural and interesting backgrounds. The use of perspective in Figs 73–75 is interesting and simple, giving an almost abstract appearance.

Many of these pictures have backgrounds that act as suspending threads so that they can hang from rods and require no background material. These suspension threads are part of the design: tree fronds in the girl and the horse and flowers, Torchon net and Bedfordshire spiders for the girl and peacocks.

Sometimes these backgrounds are drawn by eye, and sometimes they can be graphed. An interesting use of the circle can give different 'sun' effects, as in Diag. 109. The positioning of the centre can change the whole appearance. This has been used in Bridget Cook's Adam and Eve picture (Fig. 00) to great effect.

The following photographs show buildings with interesting backgrounds.

Diag. 109

Fig. 74   Gothic Prague *(15cm × 35cm) by Marie Jarkovska*

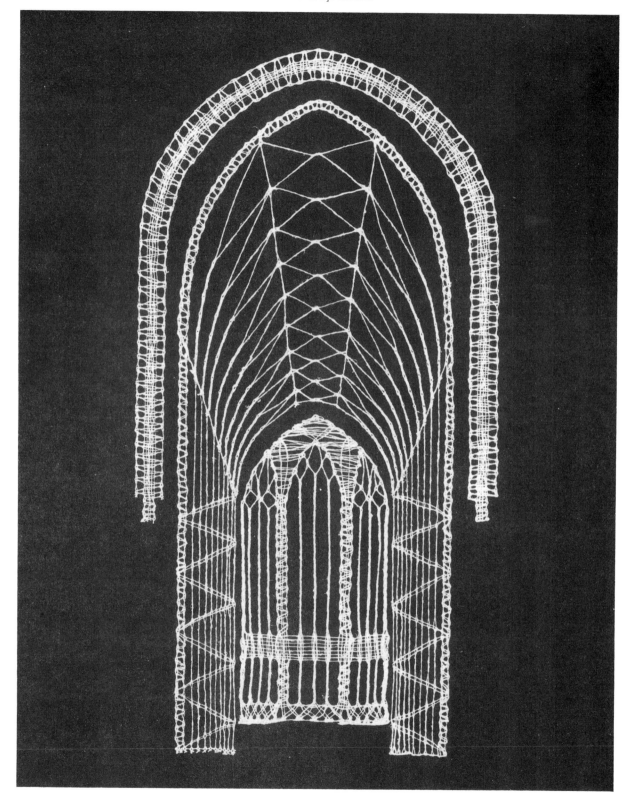

Fig. 75 Gothic Prague *(15cm × 35cm) by Marie Jar-kovska*

Fig. 76 Deliberated Prague *(1.40m × 1.25m) by Marie Vankova Kuchynkova worked in white and gold by M. Bzonkova*

Fig. 77 Prague *(1.20m × 1.5m) by Marie Jarkovska*

Fig. 78 Prague in Flowers *by Marie Vankova Kuchynkova (1.60m × 1.15m) worked in natural linen by Jana Stefkova*

Fig. 79 The Singing Fountain *by Marie Vankova* **Fig. 80** *Detail of Fig. 79*
Kuchynkova (95cm × 80cm)

Fig. 81 Baroque Prague *(20cm × 30cm) by Marie Jarkovska*

Fig. 82 *Tablecloth with lace made as a continuation of the cloth through removing the weft threads and using the remainder to work the lace (1.20m × 0.60m) in white and natural linen worked; by Marie Vankova Kuchynkova*

Modern bobbin lace

Bobbin lace is beginning to emerge as a modern art form particularly in the Eastern European countries and in some of the hitherto traditional lacemaking areas of Belgium and France. Simple lacemaking techniques are used to produce very new modern interpretations: some are large architectural constructions while others are very small miniature textiles.

Modern art endeavours to convey a feeling or an impression: the aesthetic qualities are important whatever the medium used. Modern lacemakers have tried to follow this principle. Lace is an open fabric of delicate transparency and many of the modern pieces retain this. Not everyone can work in this way or even have any desire to do so but the growth of modern design is nevertheless an important development in the lace field.

As we move forwards the twenty-first century, lacemaking will probably take the same course as embroidery. The techniques have always been there; some people become artists in the medium and develop their own designs, but the vast majority rely on transfers and printed charts or work from kits, and so it is with lace. The lace pricking can be compared with the transfer; there are many books on the various lace techniques with patterns and instructions to follow and for many people this is sufficient. However, there are those, perhaps more ambitious, who want to make their own designs. New thread textures may be used but the traditional techniques do not change, and it is important to realize that one cannot be a good designer without first learning the basics. The more techniques one can master the easier it is to interpret drawn designs, or create new ones.

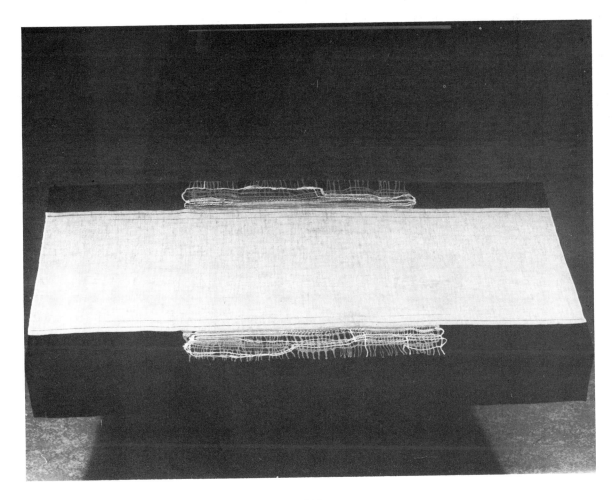

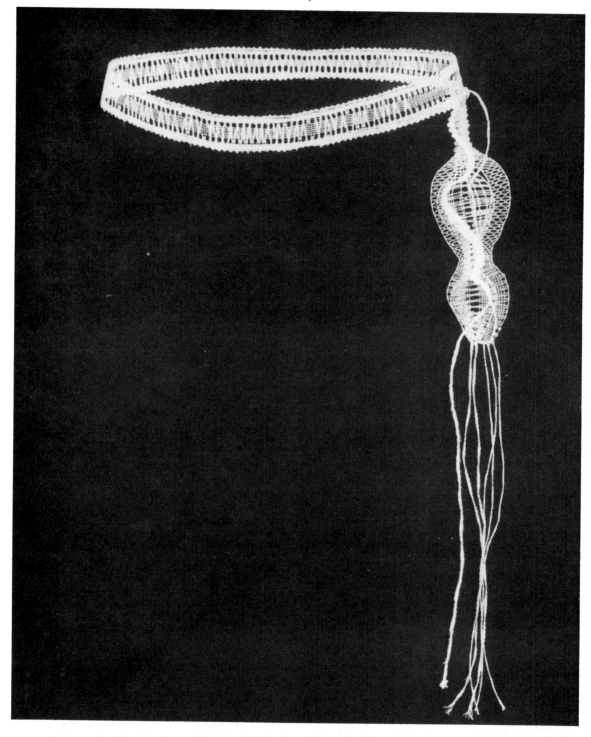

Fig. 83 *Maxi earring in white, natural and gold by Marie Vankova Kuchynkova*

Fig. 84 *Tie-like necklace in white, natural and gold by Marie Vankova Kuchynkova*

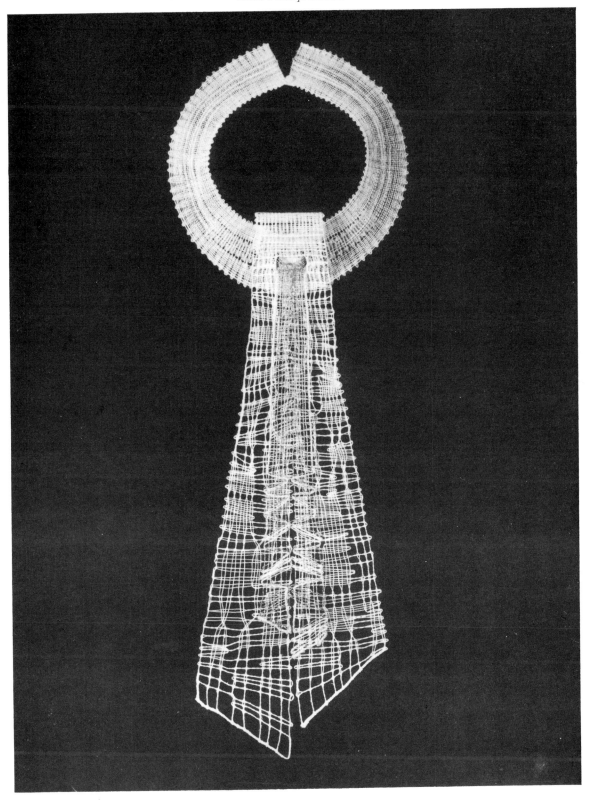

Fig. 85 Peace *(2m × 1m) by Marie Vankova Kuchyn-* **Fig. 86** *Detail of Fig. 85*
kova, worked by Jana Stefkova

Fig. 87 Tree *by B. Hanusova*

Fig. 88 *Miniature textile,* The
Last Flower *(12cm × 10cm) in
coloured linen threads, white, green,
yellow, khaki and brown, by Marie
Vankova Kuchynkova*

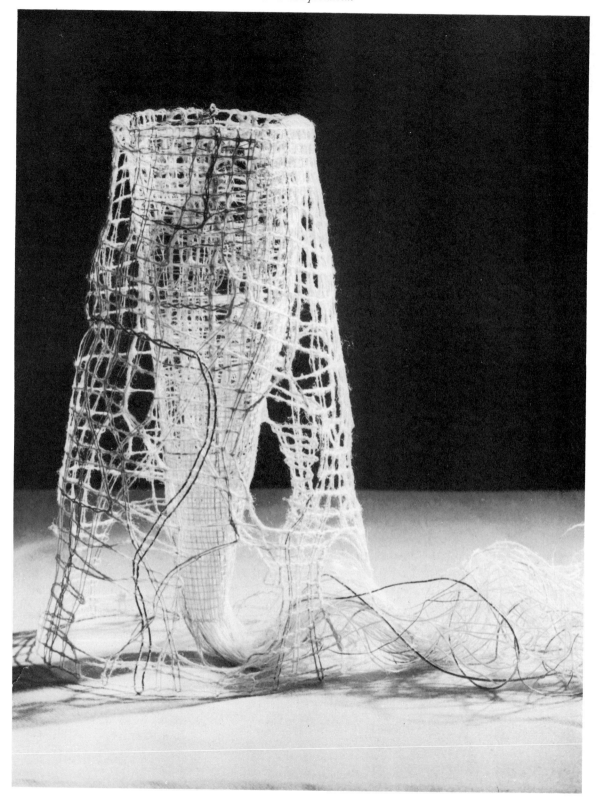

Fig. 89 Double Pyramid *in white, natural, silver and gold (17cm × 10cm) by Marie Vankova Kuchynkova*

Fig. 90 Spinner's Work, *lace miniature (17cm × 20cm) by Marie Vankova Kuchynkova*

SEVEN

Useful hints

Colour

As you will see from the coloured butterfly (page 113), mixing coloured threads is very similar to mixing colours on a palette: many of the same rules apply. Many people have difficulty with colour although they can recognize harmony or discord and have certain preferences in colour combination. When making lace one needs to know in advance what colours will blend and what is likely to be harmonious and effective. When using colour for the first time, it is advisable to use a limited palette with only one or two colours, or shades of one colour. Lace often looks better in soft pale shades rather than the full hue. Rainbow-variegated threads are sometimes suitable but the range and randomness of the colours mean that one cannot plan them, and the resulting pattern can be garish.

The weaver pair will dominate the colour scheme although some results are surprising: for example, pink through yellow gives orange, but pink through white will be pink.

Colour terms

Hues are colours of full intensity.
Tints are hues mixed with white.
Shades are hues mixed with black.
Neutrals are in the range white through grey to black.
Complementary colours lie opposite one another on the colour wheel.
Warm colours are in the range yellow through red to purple.
Cold colours are in the range yellow through green and blue to purple.
Discordant colours are the ones which are not pleasing to the eye.
Harmonious colours are pleasing and can be:
  Adjacent to one another on the wheel.
  Two shades or tints of the same colour.
  Two complementary colours.

The colour wheel

Make a colour wheel from Diag. 110. Colour in the wheel as indicated: yellow, orange-red, red, cerise, magenta, purple; and yellow, yellow-green, green, turquoise, blue, deep blue, purple. Mount the wheel on card and cut out; make another, inner wheel and mount. Pin the two together on a board and try the colours.

Pin stitch

This is sometimes referred to as single hem stitch and is a very neat and strong method of attachment. Tack the lace into position and work the stitches in the following order (Diag. 111): bring the needle up through the material and the lace and insert back through the material below the edge of the lace, taking a quarter-inch stitch. Repeat this stitch, drawing the thread tight. Insert in the second hole as shown and bring out through the material and lace to begin another complete stitch.

Triangle or punch stitch

This is much stronger than pin stitch and one can cut back to it. Tack the lace into position as before and pull the thread tight after each stitch. The numbers on Diag. 112 show the sequence of stitches. Insert the needle at 1 and bring out at 2; repeat this stitch. Insert at 3 and at 2. Insert at 3 and out at 4; repeat this stitch. Insert at 2 and out at 4; insert at 2 and out at 5. Continue this keeping the triangle formation.

Glueing threads

Sometimes the thread is very slippery as in silk or rayon and after sewing in and cutting off the threads could come undone (this does not occur with cotton

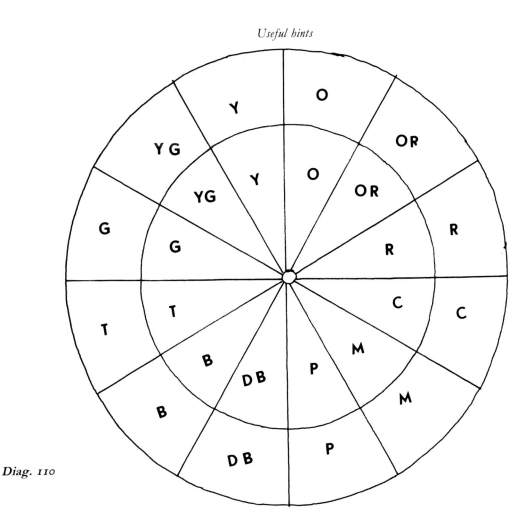

Diag. 110

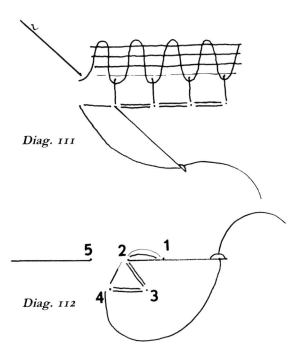

Diag. 111

Diag. 112

and linen thread). Put a tiny pin point of glue on the knot and it can then be cut very close. Use a clear-drying glue. This method is not suitable if a garment is to be washed.

Silk threads (single filament)

This thread is easier to use if it is wound on to bobbins through beeswax. Spun silk does not need this treatment.

Sewings

There are two kinds of sewings: one where the weaver is sewn into the pinhole loop and one where it is sewn into the bars on each side of the pinhole (top sewings). Use top sewings for fillings and where a sewing is needed more than once in the same place.

Sewings can be done with a fine crochet hook, a needlepin or a wig hook but there are two other methods for difficult sewings.

Needle-eye method

Place a fine needle into a cork or wood handle with the eye to the outside. Thread with a coloured thread and pull it so that the thread is double. Push the eye through the loop or bar of the lace (Diag. 113) and pull the thread through to make a loop. Put the weaver through this loop and gently pull the needle back through the lace, bringing the bobbin thread with it. Continue as usual for a sewing.

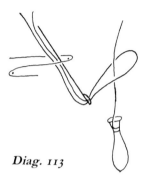

Diag. 113

Magic thread

This is useful for a difficult sewing but has to be planned in advance (Diag. 114). Fold a piece of coloured thread in half and insert it under the weavers when they are pinned up for the first time and leave it in position until a sewing is required into that stitch. Place the weaver to be sewn in through the loop of the thread and gently pull the weaver thread through. This needs to be planned in advance since this thread is placed in the pinhole that is to be sewn into. It is particularly useful for turning on a pin for scrolls or rounds, or for any other difficult part.

The rule for sewing in is: when sewing in to the left, take the top bobbin through and pass the under one through it right to left; when sewing into the right, take the lower bobbin through and pass the upper one through it right to left. This forms a continuity and the sewing is then part of a normal stitch.

Diag. 114

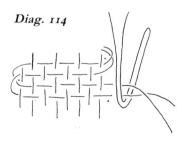

Matching threads to prickings

If a braid is made without preprickings, the pin should be placed where the weaving thread lies comfortably across. After a few rows a definite comfortable distance will evolve; use this to mark the rest of the holes.

Diag. 115 shows the different spacings of dots and it all depends on how close or how open you want the lace to be.

A For one-ply wool, *coton à broder*, cordonnet 60 to 100, 35 linen, 40 to 60 crochet cotton, 3 to 6 strands of Anchor stranded cotton.

B Close grounds with the threads from **A**, more open ones with 40 to 50 linen, 2 strands of Anchor stranded, DMC 20, Sylko 36, Coats Italian 30 and Fil à Dentelle.

C Close grounds with the threads from **B**, more open ones with 50 linen, Sylko 40, DMC 30.

D Close grounds with the threads from **C**, more open with Sylko 50, one-strand Anchor, 90 to 100 linen and DMC 50.

E 120 to 180 Honiton thread, 120 to 150 linen and DMC 60 to 100.

Graph papers and grids

Graph paper marked out for Torchon circles; six of these will make a circle (Diag. 116).
Graph paper marked for Torchon or Bucks suitable for a large circle; 18 make a complete circle (Diag. 117).
Graph paper marked out for fine Bucks; six make a complete circle (Diag. 118).
Graph paper circle (Diag. 119).
Unusual graph paper which has many uses in design; it was used for the tail of the stylized peacock (Fig. 73; Diag. 120).

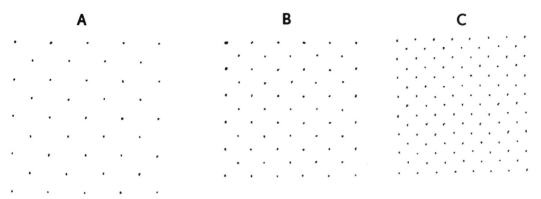

A **B** **C**

D **E** **F**

Diag. 115

Diag. 116

Diag. *117*

Diag. *118*

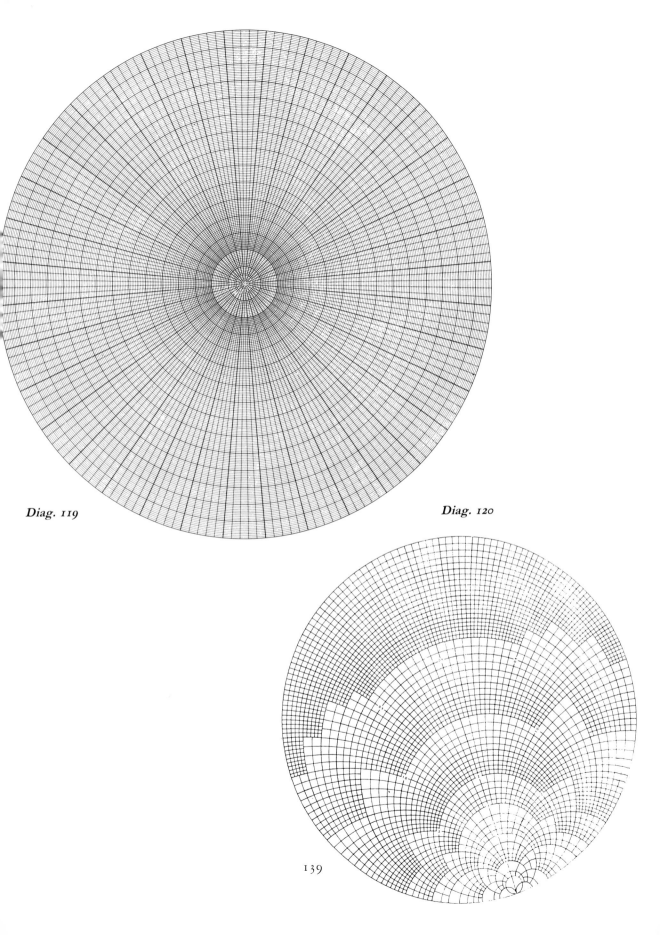

Diag. 119

Diag. 120

139

Sources of design

There is no limit to the range of sources of design inspiration. Here are just a few, which have proved useful in the author's experience. Let your imagination lead you to others.

Historical

Manuscript illuminations
Egyptian tomb paintings
Pottery decoration
Textile decoration
Oriental carpets
Cave paintings
Brass rubbings
Antique lace
Stained glass
Jacobean crewel embroidery
Cross stitch samplers
Folk art

Natural

Plants
leaves
grasses
flowers
ferns
trees
fruit
seed heads
animals
insects
fish
birds
seaweed
shells
molecular structures
reflections
bark rubbings
snowflakes
frost patterns
leaf and fish skeletons
waterfalls

Others

Greetings cards
Magazine illustrations
Children's art
Wrought iron
Chinese paper cuts
Abstract oil-on-water patterns
Illustrated book covers
Wallpaper

Useful books for inspiration

ALLAN, Mea   *The Family of Flowers*   Pitman 1979
ARMSTRONG, Nancy   *Fans – A Collector's Guide*   Souvenir 1984
CONNELL, Patrick   *Greek Ornament*   Batsford 1968
COOK, Bridget and STOTT, Geraldine   *Introduction to Bobbin Lace Stitches*   Batsford 1983
DOUGLAS, Winsome   *Toys for Your Delight*   Mills and Boon
EIRWEN-JONES, Mary   *English Crewel Designs*   Macdonald
GILLON, Edmund Vincent   *Art Nouveau*   Dover 1970
GILLON, Edmund Vincent   *Geometric Design and Ornament*   Dover 1970
GRAFTON, Carol B.   *Decorative Alphabets for Needleworkers, Craftsmen and Artists*   Dover 1982
HAECKEL, Ernst   *Art Forms in Nature*   Dover 1974
HARLOW, William M.   *Art Forms from Plant Life*   Dover 1977
MCDOWELL, Pamela   *Pressed Flower Collages and Other Ideas*   Lutterworth
MADSEN, J. M.   *Aquarium Fishes in Colour*   Macmillan
MENTEN, Theodore   *Chinese Cut Paper Designs*   Dover 1976
MESSENT, Jan   *Embroidery and Animals*   Batsford 1984
MESSENT, Jan   *Embroidery and Nature*   Batsford 1980
MIROW, Gregory   *Treasury of Design for Artists and Craftsmen*   Dover 1969
NICHOLS, Marion   *Designs and Patterns for Embroiderers and Craftsmen*   Dover 1973
SIBBETT, Ed. (Jnr)   *Floral Stained Glass Pattern Book*   Dover 1982
ZAHRADNIK, Jiri   *Field Guide in Colour to Insects*   Octopus 1978

Sources of general information

For information on all aspects of lace write to:

The Lace Guild
The Hollies
53 Audnam
Stourbridge
West Midlands DY8 4AE

International Old Lacers
P.O. Box 1029
Westminster
Colorado 80030
USA

Kantcentrum
Balstraat 14
8000 Brugge
Belgium

Centre D'Initiation
 à la dentelle du Puy
2 rue Duguesclin
4300 Le Puy
France

Lace supplies

U.K.

Win Sargent
Cottage Crafts
3 High Heavens Wood
Marlow Bottom
Bucks SL7 3QQ

D. J. Hornsby
149 High Street
Burton Latimer
Kettering
Northants NN15 5RL

Mace and Nairn
89 Crane Street
Salisbury
Wiltshire SP1 2PY

Bryn Phillips
'Pantglas'
Cellan Lampeter
Dyfed SA48 8JD

Christine and David Springett
21 Hillmorton Road
Rugby
Warwickshire CV22 5DF

George White
Delaheys
Thistle Hill
Knaresborough North Yorkshire

Dorothy Pearce
5 Fulshaw Avenue
Wilmslow Cheshire

Valley house Craft Studio
Ruston
Scarborough
North Yorkshire

Jack Piper
'Silverlea'
Flax Lane
Glemsford
Suffolk CO10 7RS
(Silk threads)

Stephen Simpson
Avenham Road Works
Preston Lancs
(gold and tinsel threads)

A. Sells
49 Pedley Lane
Clifton
Sheffield
Bedfordshire

USA

Berga Ullman Inc
PO Box 918
North Adams
Mass. 01247

Frederick J. Fawcett
129 South Street
Boston Mass.

Osma G. Tod Studio
319 Mendoza Avenue
Coral Gables
Florida 33134

Robin and Russ Handweavers
533 North Adams Street
McMinnville
Oregon 97128

Lacis
2990 Adeline Street
Berkley
California 94703

Happy Hands
3007 S. W. Marshall
Pendleton
Oregon 97108

Frivolité
15526 Densmore N.
Seattle
Washington 98133

Belgium

Manufacture Belge de Dentelle
6 Galerie de la Reine
Galeries Royales St Hubert
1000 Bruxelles

Index